Praise for

Upside Down in the Yukon River

"Steve is one of an elite bunch of crazy athletes...They dream big and believe that life is not meant to be lived at half throttle but to be lived 'all in.' Steve is one of those rare characters, and this book will enthrall."

— LISA TAMATI, professional ultra endurance athlete, author of two international bestselling books, motivational speaker, and running and mindset coach

"Steve...convey[s] the details of his adventures in a way that captivates and entertains. He shares the excitement, danger, and even...mundane aspects of ultra racing with humor and real human emotion. His books fuel the drive to continue to seek out and find my own adventures in life."

— SARAH COOPER, 2017 Race Across America winner

"This book is a must-read for all adventure seekers and all who love to live life to the fullest...Everyone should take a leaf out of Steve's book about the importance of grabbing the moment. The book is beautifully written and difficult to put down."

— CARL CLINTON, world record-holder—London to Paris Rowing Challenge and 2008 Yukon River Quest Champion Men's Pairs, Kayak Class

"Steve's writing really makes you feel like you are on the journey with him...This book is for anyone [who wants] to get up 'off the couch' and just do something. Steve helps you realize life is worth living to the best of your potential."

—JOYCE HAGLEY, Register's Annual Great Bicycle Ride Across Iowa alumna, yoga enthusiast, kayaker, and paddleboarder

"What a great read...I had to sit outside and read it. Seemed a crime to not be breathing fresh air while inhaling every moment. Wow...brilliant."

—RONALD M. SHERGA, Rocky Racoon Endurance Trail Run finisher and founder of EcoStrate

"A staggering journey that will lift your soul and make you want to test your own limits. This book shows what is possible, with an unerring belief in one's self and a drive to [not just] live life but experience it. Steve will inspire you to try harder."

—BRIAN D. MEEKS, author of the Henry Wood Detective series

"I wasn't prepared for the impact Upside Down on the Yukon River would have on me. The kayaker in me was excited to read about his adventure in the longest kayak race in the world...The mother in me was deeply moved by his words. The adventurer in me was awakened, my human spirit encouraged and uplifted by his insightfulness about life and its struggles and triumphs."

—LORI MONEY, ultra mother and 14ers hiker

"Steve Cannon's Upside Down in the Yukon River takes one on a very exciting and thrilling journey, detailing his story of adventure and survival. Intensely compelling read. Couldn't put it down."

—SYLVIA BORK, Steve's very biased mother

"As an adventure-seeker myself, I could not put the book down…I was captivated by Steve's incredible mental, physical, and spiritual capacity. Steve's journey is, without a doubt, one of the most remarkable experiences of perseverance and grit in action!"

—LISA SMITH-BATCHEN, adventurer and endurance athlete, endurance coach and teacher, motivational speaker, and race director

"The day arrived, and the postman left the package. I wasn't disappointed. The book was fantastic!"

—ROB CASSIN, world record-holder—London to Paris Rowing Challenge and 2008 Yukon River Quest Champion Men's Pairs, Kayak Class

UPSIDE DOWN

DOWN

IN THE

YUKON RIVER

UPSIDE DOWN

DOWN

IN THE

YUKON RIVER

Adventure, Survival, and the World's Longest Kayak Race

STEVE CANNON

www.expandyourpossible.com

First Edition
Printed in the United States of America

Cover and book design by Vinnie Kinsella
Cover illustration by Gene Hamilton

ISBN: 978-1-7328531-0-2
eBook ISBN: 978-1-7328531-1-9
Kindle ISBN: 978-1-7328531-2-6
Audiobook ISBN: 978-1-7328531-3-3

For information about special discounts for bulk purchases or booking the
author for an event, please visit www.expandyourpossible.com.

UPSIDE DOWN IN THE YUKON RIVER

For cancer fighters, dreamers, and believers everywhere.

The Spell of The Yukon

I wanted the gold, and I sought it;
    I scrabbled and mucked like a slave.
Was it famine or scurvy—I fought it;
    I hurled my youth into a grave.
I wanted the gold, and I got it—
    Came out with a fortune last fall—
Yet somehow life's not what I thought it,
    And somehow the gold isn't all.

No! There's the land. (Have you seen it?)
    It's the cussedest land that I know,
From the big, dizzy mountains that screen it
    To the deep, deathlike valleys below.
Some say God was tired when He made it;
    Some say it's a fine land to shun;
Maybe; but there's some as would trade it
    For no land on earth—and I'm one.

You come to get rich (damned good reason);
    You feel like an exile at first;
You hate it like hell for a season,
    And then you are worse than the worst.
It grips you like some kinds of sinning;
    It twists you from foe to a friend;
It seems it's been since the beginning;
    It seems it will be to the end.

I've stood in some mighty-mouthed hollow
    That's plumb-full of hush to the brim;
I've watched the big, husky sun wallow
    In crimson and gold, and grow dim,
Till the moon set the pearly peaks gleaming,
    And the stars tumbled out, neck and crop;
And I've thought that I surely was dreaming,
    With the peace o' the world piled on top.

The summer—no sweeter was ever;
    The sunshiny woods all athrill;
The grayling aleap in the river,
    The bighorn asleep on the hill.
The strong life that never knows harness;
    The wilds where the caribou call;
The freshness, the freedom, the farness—
    O God! how I'm stuck on it all.

The winter! the brightness that blinds you,
    The white land locked tight as a drum,
The cold fear that follows and finds you,
    The silence that bludgeons you dumb.
The snows that are older than history,
    The woods where the weird shadows slant;
The stillness, the moonlight, the mystery,
    I've bade 'em good-by—but I can't.

There's a land where the mountains are nameless,
    And the rivers all run God knows where;
There are lives that are erring and aimless,
    And deaths that just hang by a hair;
There are hardships that nobody reckons;
    There are valleys unpeopled and still;
There's a land—oh, it beckons and beckons,
    And I want to go back—and I will.

They're making my money diminish;
    I'm sick of the taste of champagne.
Thank God! when I'm skinned to a finish
    I'll pike to the Yukon again.
I'll fight—and you bet it's no sham-fight;
    It's hell!—but I've been there before;
And it's better than this by a damsite—
    So me for the Yukon once more.

There's gold, and it's haunting and haunting;
    It's luring me on as of old;
Yet it isn't the gold that I'm wanting
    So much as just finding the gold.
It's the great, big, broad land 'way up yonder,
    It's the forests where silence has lease;
It's the beauty that thrills me with wonder,
    It's the stillness that fills me with peace.

—"The Spell of the Yukon," ROBERT W. SERVICE

Chapter 1

I FELT NO PANIC, NO FEAR—WHICH WOULD HAVE SEEMED ODD to anyone witnessing my dilemma from the riverbank. I was upside down in the Yukon River, trapped in my kayak and unable to get free.

Racers were warned that this lake, Lake Laberge, had ended many lives because of its size and unstable weather patterns. The entire week leading up to the event that brought me there hadn't been any different; for the most part, the weather had sucked. It had been an unseasonably cold and wet spring in this part of the Yukon Territory; in most years, the sun was a more constant companion by June, and the spring rains had waned. Even in the warmest and most stable years, however, it was commonplace for an afternoon storm to whip the lake into a frenzy, dump those in its way, and then disappear, content with the havoc it had wreaked. This was where DNFs ("did not finish") were made.

More than forty-two kilometers long, Lake Laberge was a wide spot in the Yukon River that stretched nearly four miles side to side. Very seldom was the year that someone didn't end up capsized there, which was exactly where I found myself at that moment. Most who made it across the lake made it to the next checkpoint; nearly 87 percent of the people who made that checkpoint finished the race. I hoped only to get free of the kayak before it became my waterlogged coffin.

I had been surfing ever-increasing swells for an hour before I'd been overturned. I reflected back to the prerace meeting. It was mandated that all of us taking on the Yukon River Quest remain within a quarter-mile of the shore. This was the rule for a couple of reasons. First, if your kayak or canoe capsized, it would be possible to get yourself to shore before hypothermia killed you. Second, the further from shore you were, the bigger the waves. Kayaking back home in Iowa had provided little opportunity—OK, zero opportunity—to practice whitecap paddling like this.

Fear could be a good thing at times, and certainly, this was one of those times. But there was also a balance to be struck. Thirty miles to get across this beast was the distance "as the crow flies." As the crow flies meant point to point, and that meant straight down the middle of the lake; which was not an option. The seemingly serene waters were as misleading as fool's gold. Much like the gold rush that drew explorers here at the turn of the century, danger or worse waited for those who did not give this place its due respect. The event rules made it clear that the quarter-mile-from-shore limit was non-negotiable. And, if caught too far from shore, you would be scolded by the race officials. Ignore their scolding, and you would be disqualified. The race directors had ample stories to justify their rules. With waves on the lake now three feet and growing, I was about to become one of their stories.

Chapter 2

ECO-CHALLENGE WAS MARK BURNETT'S BABY, THE BEGINNING of reality TV, the genre that eventually led to the Kardashian family's media empire. I'm sure that was a completely unintended consequence. Burnett's show detailed the racing adventures of four-person teams from around the globe in some of the most remote, gnarly, nasty, beautiful areas of our planet.

Two stints living in Colorado had opened my eyes to the adventure/endurance athlete scene. *Eco-Challenge* was irresistible, and I was practically addicted to it. I could feel it. The more remote the adventure, the higher the suffering these nutjob super-athletes faced, the more I jonesed for it.

The Aussie team would attempt to stay awake for the entire race—something insane like five days—and eventually one of their members nearly walked off a cliff in a sleep-deprived haze. One of the women from the all-women team cut her finger lashing a makeshift boat together. Seemingly innocuous at the time, days later the infection from that cut nearly killed her. Three teammates tried to nurse their fourth along as he fought giardia—puking in the boat, out of the boat, and occasionally on himself and any-thing or anyone else within the blast range. This was the eclipse I couldn't help but look into. All for one and one for all! No per-son left behind! Either you all finished or no one finished. Four working together as one.

The show captivated all who watched it. It was the stuff you talked about the next day at the coffee shop or the water cooler.

Ian Adamson, Robyn Benincasa, Rebecca Rusch, Marshall Ulrich: these people became my sports heroes. Mark Burnett gave me the fix I needed, giving me episode after episode for free, knowing I'd return for more. Pretty soon, I wanted something more than simply observing these people put their survivor skills to the test every week while I went on quietly with the rest of my life.

I wanted in.

Chapter 3

Adventure racing introduced me to paddling. Like most kids, I had spent a bit of time in a canoe growing up—not much, though. The only real memory was a family trip to northwest Iowa. My cousin Brian and I had paddled out to a small island, maybe a mile or so from camp. The water was calm, and a slight breeze at our back made the trip a real treat. Brian had some paddling experience; he and his father had taken a few trips to the Boundary Waters Canoe Area Wilderness in Minnesota. I believe this was my maiden voyage.

They gave me a few basic pointers, explaining how your hand goes on top of the paddle, the best way to slip your paddle into the water, and the proper exit point. A few strokes on your left, a few on the right, repeat. Brian would handle keeping us on course from the rear of the boat. There was no mention of fore, aft, starboard, or port. Maiden canoe voyages were the stuff of left, right, front, and back.

Arriving at the little island, we were Sir Edmund Hillary, Roald Amundsen, Neil Armstrong—great explorers. The first to set foot on this faraway land. Beaching our aluminum vessel, stepping into the clear, chilly, bluish-green waters, and steadying the boat for my trusted companion, I was feeling quite full of myself. There was an innocence to it, though, a sort of self-amazement: *Did I really just paddle from that distant shore to here? Me, the city kid, who reluctantly came along on this trip in the first place?*

Per Brian's instructions, I steadied the boat, watching as he stepped slowly and deliberately down the center of our vessel so he wouldn't topple it. As he exited the front of the canoe, we pulled the now much-lighter craft onto the beach. Time to explore our newfound island. Wonder filled me and questions raced through my head. *What might lurk beyond the small sandy beach we stood on? Were bears hiding beyond our view? Are there bears in Iowa?* As I was fairly certain there weren't, it felt a bit like the bogeyman. Of course, in the safety and light of day, the bogeyman is a silly concept. But when darkness falls and you hear a bump in the night, suddenly what seemed so silly an hour ago has a bit more teeth. This felt similar. Bears were an almost-laughable idea from the distant shore—but we were no longer on the distant shore. This was uncharted territory, and once we were among the towering trees, who knew what dangers lurked?

Brian took the lead as we began our exploration. Armed with "machetes" made of found tree branches, we were prepared for all matters of bushwhacking and, if necessary, self-defense. Young minds are such fertile ground. Just add adventure and watch what sprouts. We were certain an indigenous tribe called this place home, and we hoped to be the first to encounter them. Brian joked that hopefully they were not of the headhunting variety. We were almost certain they would not be, but even if they were, a couple of young kids' heads would probably be of little trophy value. We were more excited by the possibilities of witnessing a tribal dance, meeting a medicine man, and returning back to camp with painted faces and necklaces proving our honorary status within the tribe.

The island was a lush environment. The forest canopy shielded much of the sky, which, unbeknownst to us, was beginning to cloud a bit. I hoped Brian was paying attention to our steps, as I realized I had been following him aimlessly and the forest didn't offer a clear path to guide our return. Being the rookie of the crew, I was not going to question his plans or abilities. My thoughts were interrupted as he stopped suddenly, his gaze intently focused just into the trees to the right.

"No way! Look at that!" he exclaimed, running a few quick steps, as if whatever "it" was might escape.

As Brian reached down to retrieve his great find, I could see an ivory-white tip just above the tall grass of the forest floor. The skull was a perfect white, bleached by the sun for who knows how long, and the eight antlers—four per side—were almost perfectly symmetrical. What a score this was! Proof of our adventure, and more importantly, evidence that we were clearly explorers of the highest degree. Brian put the beast's skull above his head like a ceremonial headdress. We concocted stories of the animal's demise. Perhaps the carcass was still near, hidden by the beast that had slain it. If so, we shouldn't dally long, or we'd risk a similar fate. Could it be that the tribe had hunted the great buck, interested only in its meat and skins for subsistence? I recalled my stepfather, a great hunter in his own right, saying while field-dressing a nice fat doe, "You can't eat the horns, son." Or had they seen our arrival from the distant shore and left the headdress as a gift, a sign of peace and welcome to the young explorers? We especially liked that idea.

We decided after lengthy discussion and celebration of our monumental find that it would be best not to overstay our welcome. We would return the gift of the island people by searching no further and leaving them in peace.

The gods of the sky had been quite busy during our exploration. The light, wispy clouds that earlier had been friendly and dancing across the light blue sky had been overtaken by darker invaders.

We wondered if we had overstayed our welcome, perhaps angering the gods that kept watch over this place.

Seasoned paddlers we were not. To be fair, I was not. We were, however, able to discern that we needed to get our butts back across that lake, pronto. Pulling the canoe from its hiding place among the lush, waist-high grasses, we readied it to go. Even a rookie kid like me knew instinctively that the small waves and stiffening wind, now in our face, were not ideal. Sticking the front half of the canoe into the water, Brian urged me in and steadied the boat so we didn't topple over. I baby-stepped my way down the center, bending slightly at the waist, enabling me to balance a bit easier as I held onto the sides of the canoe. Once I'd found my seat in the front, Brian launched us with a few quick steps in the now not-so-friendly waters. He hopped in, taking his seat at the rear.

Brian's instructions were clear before we were underway: three strokes left, three strokes right, repeat. Rest if you have to, but it would be best if you didn't so we don't go backward. I understood. Our lighthearted adventure was on hold. The dark clouds above had sent an invitation to the winds, and they had gratefully accepted. In turn, the lake was being churned up, its waves pushing back against our every stroke. Earlier, the slight breeze and currents maximized the distance travelled each time our paddles pulled the water below. This was no longer the case; it was as if the island or its unseen inhabitants were willing us back. The sun-drenched buck's skull, now on the canoe floor between us, may not have been a gift after all. It seemed like something wanted it back.

Brian was doing expert work keeping us in line. We would beat slightly left by the third strike on the right side of the boat, coming back in line as I switched my paddling to the left. On occasion, we would get a bit off-kilter and, in doing so, nearly tip as the waves would catch us on the side. Sure, we had our life jackets on, but I didn't know one thing about self-rescue. The thought of tipping scared me as the cold water below splashed up on us with every rogue wave. Brian hollered a word or two of encouragement from time to time. I'm not sure if he was frightened more by the predicament we were in or if he knew I really had no idea what I was doing. The latter probably exacerbated the former. Closing in on the shore provided a bit of relief from the wind, which in turn began to settle the water. A slight rain had begun. We paid it little mind though, relieved by the fact that we may actually return to terra firma mostly dry. The canoe hissed as it reached the end of our journey, its bottom rubbing against the sand below. It was a welcome sound.

The return paddle from the island, somehow escaping the lake's wrath, had taken us about an hour or so. I crumpled over myself, equal parts exhausted and relieved. Brian, in his haste to get us back as quickly as possible, had shot for the nearest land, which put us a good bit from camp, where we had initially launched. I had noticed this when I'd take a rare moment to look up from my three-stroke-left, three-stroke-right pattern, but it didn't cross my mind to question my navigator. I had simple instructions, and I had been pretty scared. I was all for anything that got us back to land as quickly as possible. The fear of capsizing or drowning was a great motivator to paddle on as told in whatever direction Brian saw fit.

Wobbly legged as could be, I exited the canoe, pulling it as far onto shore as I was able to make it easier for Brian to get out. We were whipped, probably a mile or so from camp, and definitely overdue to return. I was about to get my second big lesson of the day: how to portage.

The main thing you need know about portaging a canoe is that it's way harder than paddling one. At least it was for two twelve-year-olds, each not strong enough to support the craft without the other's help. Thinking back on the scene, I'm reminded of an old saying: "It looked like two monkeys trying to have sex with a football." Even if we weren't already exhausted and were on our best day, on flat pavement, and dealing with no overhanging branches, rocks underfoot, or ninety-degree turns, carrying that aluminum craft a mile would have sucked. It would have made a roaring silent picture, sped up and accompanied by the music of the Keystone Cops: take three steps, bang into a tree, switch shoulders, drop the canoe on your foot, curse using words twelve-year-olds aren't supposed to know—thankfully it's a silent movie—take four more steps, stumble, fall while trying to look ahead so as to not hit another tree head-on, more cursing. What a comedy of errors! It would be funny only to those who might have been watching. There was no humor in this at all for us. I was a soft city kid, in over my head, and Brian, although more seasoned, was still barely ninety pounds all in.

Continuing down the trail, keeping the shore in sight as best we could to serve as our guide, we finally broke through, emerging from the woods that had held us captive. We dropped the canoe and fell to our knees. We had made it—almost. The family site was still at the other end of the campground. It was OK, though; the canoe could be dragged from here. It would have to be anyway, since the craft had somehow become a hundred pounds heavier in the past few hours.

Lugging the canoe into camp those last few steps felt like a cruel joke. The angry skies were calm once more. Everyone looked curious, wondering why we appeared so haggard. It seemed we were barely missed. Didn't they notice the wind that whipped the lake into a boiling sea, bent on keeping us as a trophy of its own? Hadn't they even questioned the whereabouts or safety of their two young explorers? The expected concern and the tirade of "Do you know how much trouble you're in? We have all been worried sick! Where the hell have you two been?" was disappointingly absent. We had been certain all of that would be forthcoming and now, without it, the tales of our great exploration lacked the proper lead-in.

Dropping the canoe next to the picnic table littered with beer and soda cans, Brian and I stood silently noticing how unnoticed we were. Perhaps that was just as it should be. The magnitude of our adventure surely would have been lost on them anyway. The heretofore-unexplored island, the tribesmen lurking around us without our knowledge, and the daring paddle and portage home would remain a memory between just us two boys—a grand adventure that would be recounted someday in books for sure. The gift of the island people fell to the ground as I untied it from my waist. Coming to rest near the canoe, the great buck's skull was a single clue left for those who might notice and wonder. Brian and I used what little energy we had left to find somewhere to lie down. Finding a cot in the back of Uncle Bob's pickup truck, I passed out more tired and more fulfilled than I'd ever been.

Chapter 4

WHEN I WOKE UP, MY SURROUNDINGS WERE UNFAMILIAR. I vaguely remembered being brought to this place, although I was unsure if it had been in a dream or reality. Exhaustion still clutching me tightly, eyes not yet open, I did my best to try and recall the events that had led me to this point. My attempts to piece these events together were frustrating: some pieces were clear, while others were just beyond my mind's reach.

I recalled a bit of a ruckus and being wheeled into a large, drab, *M.A.S.H.*-like tent. It seemed almost out-of-body, to my recollection—it was more like I was watching it happen than actually experiencing it. I recalled a real urgency to what I could only guess was a nurse or some medical professional's voice. She instructed that I be removed from the emergency suit, stripped of all my clothes, and warmed up—now! I couldn't remember the exact details and words; it was as if I'd become the main character in a movie with no sound. The urgency had been clear. It was surreal to be lying there, attempting to piece events together, half conscious, still unsure if any of my recollections were based in reality.

There was little more than a twinge of discomfort or embarrassment as I was taken out of the bulky orange emergency suit and stripped out of my still-damp clothing. Yes, the big orange emergency suit. I remembered. They had called for a rescue boat. Apparently the volunteer had seen I was not well as I sat next to the small fire on the shoreline, contemplating my ability to continue the race. He may have saved my life. Shortly after abandoning the race and getting on the rescue boat, I'd been instructed to put on the emergency suit. I had seen these things on TV: crab fishermen who'd fallen overboard were placed in them in an attempt to stave off hypothermia. We were miles from the halfway point, and the rescue boat captain got me into the suit immediately, offering up some hot coffee as we launched. Turns out, he also had helped save my life. Terribly disappointed to have DNFed, the orange suit seemed like a small badge of honor. It was almost cool. *Well, at least you went down swinging*, I thought. No one would question my reasons for quitting or my toughness once we arrived safely at the halfway checkpoint. My ego was doing its best to find some solace in failure, but the mental conversations and justifications would not last long. I lost consciousness shortly after.

The lone white light bulb hanging from the ceiling cast just enough light to allow those within the tent to do their work. Everything seemed random and senseless. *Why are they taking all my clothes off? What is going on? What has happened to me? Am I dreaming?* I have had those kinds of dreams, at times so vivid, certain they were reality. I remembered a warm drink, something like chicken soup, put to my lips.

"Drink this," instructed a voice from somewhere as someone held my head up. "We need to get his body temperature up quickly. He's in trouble," I remember hearing.

I was growing a bit more certain that I was indeed alive. At times it had seemed unclear, like that space in books or movies when a character watches their life pass before them. Maybe I had been in the in-between place, straddling the line dividing the living and the dead. The weight of the wool blankets piled on top of me made it difficult to move. A large stocking cap covered my head. Gaining an ever-so-slight grasp of my surroundings, I considered that had anyone entered the tent, I doubt I'd have been noticed, entombed in what nearly became my sheepskin casket. I was most assuredly alive. The wool cocoon, the headache that felt like an icepick in my forehead, the tent walls, and the faint voices coming from outside confirmed this was indeed a real place. My eyes opened for the first time. As I was still very groggy, I had no idea where "here" really was. Was it day or night? *What* day or night? Many questions needed answers. Where in the hell were my clothes?!

That seemed a logical place to start.

Chapter 5

I SAT AT THE COMPUTER. THE ROOM WASN'T LARGE, DOUBLING as both an office and a living room. Flat-screen TVs had not yet become the norm, so the faux wood-paneled TV I'd inherited from my grandfather (which I still have to this day) served as both desk and entertainment.

Adventure racing had allowed me to dip my toe into many different waters, which is the real beauty of the sport. Rappelling and ropes had appealed to my climbing side, which was where all my adventuring had begun in my late twenties. I'd travelled with my good friend Ty Dickerson to Eldorado Canyon years prior to experiencing my first rock-climbing trip—in a VW van, of course. With barely enough money for gas and some freeze-dried food, we fit the part of "dirtbag climbers," and we loved every second of it. We'd climb all day and read books all night about the great climbers like John Long and Lynn Hill. That trip in the summer of 1990 had opened my eyes to the adventurous lifestyle and mindset, and it had eventually led me to living in Colorado for a short time, where I had been introduced to all manner of adventure and adventure athletes.

Orienteering had been like learning a whole new language. I loved the idea of guiding a team through unfamiliar terrain in search of a hand-sized tent hanging from a tree limb in the dark of night. Once found, you would use the small card punch attached to prove that you had indeed been there, and as quickly and quietly as possible, you'd get the hell out of there so as not to alert other teams still in search of the same checkpoint.

My teammates and I even came up with code to signal that one of us had found the "treasure." Once certain we were in the vicinity of the checkpoint, we would fan out as nonchalantly as possible, not wanting to draw any attention, and wait to hear the signal. "Wow! Who farted?" someone would say. Genius, right? We figured it was unlikely anyone would be within earshot. But, if someone did hear us—voices do travel a long way in the woods—we gambled that nobody would think about heading our way after such a proclamation of stink. We'd play it up big, too. "Aw, dude, that's horrible! What the hell did you eat?" Dana would chime in. "This is the last time I'm racing with you guys. That's not funny. I'm gonna hurl!" All the while, we were converging on the one who supposedly had dropped the butt-bomb (the person at the checkpoint), trying not to laugh and blow our cover.

Running and cycling had also proved to be a lot of fun, but it was paddling that I had really fallen in love with. We'd bungled our first few adventure races. Not having practiced much, we were unsure of the best system. We always competed in the three-person co-ed division. Steve Giblin and Dana Kennedy rounded out our team of three. Both were fantastic athletes and, more importantly, great friends. They were tough as nails, patient, and had an ability to laugh when things got sideways. The last attribute was the most important.

Robyn Benincasa, a professional adventure racer and world champion, spoke to us before an adventure race in Chicago, saying, "Look around. It won't be the super fit-looking athletes who will win; it will be those who can work together and problem-solve the best…and have the most fun." Great advice—not just for adventure racing but also for life.

It became obvious that more paddle time was needed after our first couple of races. We didn't lack the horsepower as much as the know-how. Steve had a canoe, so we began incorporating it into our workouts. Not long after, enjoying the paddling, I invested in a sea kayak, a fourteen-footer designed to cover longer stretches of water with less resistance. The longer the kayak, the better it tracks through the water. This makes it much more responsive, but it also makes it easier to tip.

Spending more and more time on the water, it didn't take long until we dialed in our system. Steve would jump in first, with Dana and I steadying the canoe. Dana got in next, and before she'd be seated, I'd have us pushed off and underway. Steve was a horse at the front of the boat and would paddle as hard as he could on either side, switching whenever he wanted. Dana would match him, and I'd play off them both, keeping the boat on line to the target. Dana doubled as the grocery lady. Eventually we'd be in races where we would paddle for hours at a time. Dana would keep us all fed, breaking out Clif Bars and GU, keeping the engines stoked.

Paddling became our strongest discipline. On the water, we more than held our own. I loved the intensity of it and the pain of it mixed with the beauty of the lakes and the wooded shorelines. At times we navigated by moonlight. Certain paddling sections required beaching the boat, heading inland to find checkpoints, and returning back to the boat. It was exhilarating—real sharp-end-of-the-stick kinda stuff. I wanted more. More distance, more remoteness, more challenge. More, more, more.

Sitting at the makeshift TV desk in my one-bedroom apartment on 42nd Street in Des Moines, Iowa, I typed "world's longest kayak race" into the search engine. One should be careful what one searches for. Almost instantly, I had an answer to my query: the Yukon River Quest.

Chapter 6

I WAS TWENTY-EIGHT YEARS OLD AND HAD RECENTLY RELO-cated to Colorado Springs from my home in Iowa City. Other than my roommate and longtime friend Jon Madsen, I didn't know anyone. Although I was comfortable being alone, per-haps too much so, I had decided that making a few new friends, ideally female ones, would be a good idea. Every weekend in Colorado Springs, spring till fall, you could find at least a five-kilometer (5K) footrace to test yourself. Running was the deal in Colorado. Of course, there were many other popular outdoor pursuits—biking, climbing, triathlon—but seemingly everyone ran. I had no real interest in killing myself at one of these, as I hadn't run in...well, ever. I'd have preferred to sign up for a 1K. Sadly, that was not an option. But it was important to keep my eye on the prize: girls.

The St. Patty's Day 5K nearly killed me—it was thirty-three minutes of hell. More than once I thought, *I don't care what the hell she looks like, she won't be worth this suffer-fest. Running sucks!* The thin air of Manitou Springs, a beautiful little town just up the front range from Colorado Springs when it wasn't the location of my 5K torment, was not so slowly sucking the life out of me. *I wonder if anyone would notice if I just excused myself and exited stage right...or left.* Crossing the finish line, happy to be alive, I vowed never to undertake such a stupid endeavor again, no mat-ter the possible reward that may await. I didn't speak to a single girl before, during, or after the race. I made straight for the car, wanting nothing more than a shower and a couch, just hopeful that I had enough energy to get to both.

Driving home, it happened. An odd sense of unfamiliar joy began to manifest. The distance between the finish line and the apartment door was just a few miles, no more than a ten-minute drive. Stepping out of the car, stiff-legged from the day's effort, I found myself feeling a bit lighter as I turned the key in the apartment door. What the hell was happening to me? Moments later, humming a tune in the shower, it was clear that I was full-on happy. Pulling on a fresh pair of shorts, I grabbed a chocolate milk and made for the couch. Making short work of the drink, I sprawled out horizontally, resting my head on one of the oversized throw pillows. My thoughts betrayed the finish line promise I'd made just an hour earlier. *That wasn't that bad; could have been worse. 5K's a pretty long way, man. That's pretty cool...Maybe I should try another one...I wonder if I could ever go any further than that?* I slept.

Fifteen years later, I would become the second person to ever run across my home state of Iowa. Three years after that, I would circle Lake Michigan, the first person ever to do so, running 1,037 miles in forty days. Had you shared that vision with me after I had finished the run that day in Manitou Springs, I'd have been certain you'd had too many green beers at the bar.

That's the beauty of this journey we are all on. There are universal truths that apply to all things. Allow yourself to dream, and there is almost nothing beyond your grasp. The power of one step, one paddle stroke, one turn of the bike pedal is beyond measure. Ask yourself, "Can I take just one step in the direction of my dream?" It doesn't matter what the dream is. Ask yourself, "Can I?" Of course the answer is yes. The poorest man or woman can take one step toward a life of financial well-being. The most out of shape can most likely take just one step toward their first walk around the block. Now, having successfully taken that first step, ask again, "Can I take just one more step in the direction of my dream?" The answer, again, will be yes. Each step reveals the possibility of a next, allowing a vision of what lies ahead that was not possible prior. Eventually, unable to see back to where it all began, you will marvel at where that first step led you. Do not allow self-limiting beliefs to sabotage you: dream big! It isn't important that you even believe the dream is possible, only that you believe one step in that direction is possible. The next step will be revealed.

That first 5K opened the door to a lifetime of adventurous pursuits, marathoning, ultramarathoning, adventure racing, mountain biking, and long-distance kayaking. Each adventure and every accomplishment was built on the others, expanding my belief in what I was capable of—and all from running a little 5K to meet chicks.

Chapter 7

PADDLING HAD STARTED FOR ME QUITE BY HAPPENSTANCE ALL those years ago when my cousin Brian and I crossed that lake in Iowa to explore a distant island. A few summers later, my Uncle Bob, perhaps sensing a flicker of adventure in me, invited me to join him and Brian on a canoe trip to the Boundary Waters.

"Can I, Mom? Can I?" I pleaded.

She responded, "How are the grades gonna be this year? If they're good, you're good."

This wasn't great news. When it came to school, motivation had always been a problem—even more so since my parents' divorce a few years earlier. Enthusiasm and commitment for much of anything had been a struggle. The invitation from Uncle Bob lit me up a bit, and this was a surprising and positive development, as I was far from adventurous at the time. Ah, but what about Mom's inquiry into the state of my studies? That posed a bit of a dilemma. I was flunking biology—and not by just a little bit—and we were deep into the semester. There was no salvaging it. That would most likely be a deal-killer for the Boundary Waters. I was at least above water in my other classes, but a full report card of four Cs and an F would not cut it. I made a decision then that I am not proud of now. I chose "beg for forgiveness later" over "tell the truth and hope for the best."

Nearly forty years later, I still remember those crystal-clear waters. The kind of clarity that would allow an awestruck twelve-year-old from the city to recover a pair of Ray-Ban sunglasses in four feet of water, presumably lost by a paddler that preceded us in this wild place. Uncle Bob taught me how to handle a fishing pole. Young northern pike, abundant in numbers and as naive as this young caster, were all too eager to take the bait we offered. Each strike sent waves of excitement through me, and I could sense Uncle Bob's delight in it. Later in life, Uncle Bob shared with me that he had thought of me as a punk kid who would never amount to much. But on that trip, the punk kid had a look in his eyes that perhaps Uncle Bob recognized from time spent with Brian, or even from when he was a kid himself. Perhaps it took him back to a time that he saw these same Boundary Waters for the first time. I'm eternally grateful he took a chance on me. You never know what may be sleeping inside a kid's soul.

Returning home, I was certain payment would be due. While I was gone, Mom surely would have received my grades in the mail. Whatever the punishment, I was at peace with it. No penalty could undo or erase the memories of the trip. Returning to Fort Dodge, the family reunion was in full swing at Aunt Barbara's family farm. Maybe Mom had enjoyed a drink or two, or maybe she saw the glimmer in my eye and was just so glad to see her son genuinely happy. Whatever the case, after listening to a few of my stories, she said with a mischievous smile, "So glad you had a wonderful trip! We'll discuss the report card a bit later." Moms are the best. It would be some time until my next big adventure, and many more poor decisions would be made in my young life. However, a seed had been planted that would never go entirely dormant.

Decades later, I'd return to the water, clumsily attempting to keep pace with much more seasoned paddlers during our first adventure race. The goal at that time was simple: become a better paddler so as not to be left in our fellow racers' wakes. Eventually, doing so allowed me to see the possibility of becoming more than just a proficient paddler. What I could be was being revealed one step—or, in this case, one paddle stroke—at a time. I wanted to go further and see what was out there, both physically and adventurously. I began spending more and more of my available training hours alone on the lakes and rivers of Iowa. Each stroke, unknowingly, was leading me north to a land far, far away. I was in the flow, adrift, being pulled by a river current yet unknown.

Chapter 8

THERE WAS NO REASON TO BELIEVE THAT THE YUKON RIVER Quest was a possibility for me. Reading the qualifications, I was a long shot to even get in. This was nothing like signing up for a 5K to meet women. This was the "longest canoe/kayak race in the world." Self-proclaimed or not, 715 kilometers (444 miles) was a damn long way. Sitting in front of the computer perched atop Grandpa's gifted TV, I was again a boy filled with wonder and a bit of dread. This was no vacation paddle to the Boundary Waters. To be honest, the distance was entirely beyond comprehension. Were it not for the history of the race and documented finishes from years prior, I might not have believed it possible. But, I thought, if they can do it, then I can do it. Now, if I could just get in.

The race waiver confirmed this adventure should be taken seriously:

> The Yukon River Quest is a long-distance race that takes you through very rugged and isolated territory where roads and people do not exist and where dangers, including death or injury from hypothermia, drowning, bear mauling, forest fire or other acts of nature, do exist.

It continued on to say—and I'm paraphrasing here—"If the shit does hit the fan, you damn well better be able to save yourself, because it may be many, many hours until we can get to you."

My adventure resumé was on the weak end of the criteria to get in. It would take some crafty wordsmithery and, hopefully, a race director who could sense my desire to take on this monumental challenge. A handful of marathons, a couple of twenty-four-hour-plus adventure races, and a few ultras paled in comparison to most of the racer bios I read. I may have exaggerated the length of some of my training paddles.

The most recent edition of the Race to the Midnight Sun featured ninety-four teams with 236 paddlers from all around the world. Fourteen countries would be represented, including Australia, Austria, sixteen Canadian provinces/territories, fifteen different states from the United States, and even South Africa. Reading through the bios was interesting and sometimes intimidating stuff, such as the 1972 Munich Olympian and race legend Heinz Rodinger, known simply as "The Austrian," who competed and completed the Yukon River Quest while in his sixties (and still does today in his seventies). What was perhaps scarier than anything was how many of those athletes, much more qualified than I, had DNFed the previous year.

Summer months in the Yukon offered the unique opportunity to play beneath the sun until the wee hours of the morning. Darkness never totally falls over the rugged landscape during the summer solstice. The race description, including its warnings, the incredible accomplishments of so many who had raced in the past, and the picture it painted of the wildness of the venue, was intoxicating. Drunk on the possibilities of what could be, I felt time vanish. Was I worthy of a spot in the race? In resumé, no. In spirit, yes.

Chapter 9

EXCITEMENT GAVE WAY TO FEAR AND QUESTIONING. I FELT A REAL joy and sense of anticipation when considering a new challenge. When that challenge involved breaking in my passport for the first time, I felt those feelings more strongly. When it involved taking on a race where things going sideways meant I would be on my own, perhaps for twenty-four hours in a land where grizzly bears roam, all feelings were magnified. A lot. Finding this race, or it finding me, created a sense of romance as I sat mesmerized and quite comfy in front of the computer. The thoughts and images of the frigid, potentially deadly Yukon River, still mostly untouched by human's advances, captivated me. They touched something primal: a desire to test myself and to disappear into this wild land.

"I've always wanted to see the frontier...before it's gone," Kevin Costner's character in *Dances with Wolves* had said when asked why he would volunteer for a post so deep in Indian territory. It was very much the same for me. The pilot light of adventure had been relit in me a few years prior, and I planned to supply it with an abundance of fuel, assuring it would never extinguish again. I wondered if perhaps the gold rushers had felt the same pull? Clearly, there was an aspect of need and financial gain that did not exist in my attraction to this wild place. However, even with these outside factors in play, there had to have been a sense of adventure pulling these gold rushers west. The allure of gold must have come hand in hand with the desire to experience this untamed land.

The realities would prove to be far less romantic. The gold I was pursuing was intended to feed the soul, not the bank account. I hoped, like those miners from so long ago had also hoped, it would not be a fool's gold. It was entirely possible I was in over my head and didn't realize it. Opening up my email and reading the confirmation that they had actually accepted my application into the world's longest kayak race, I was hit by that very thought with the pragmatism of a cold northern wind. Romance suddenly took a backseat to reality.

My palms began to get clammy, my stomach soured, and my mind began to chirp. The battle was on. Devil on my left shoulder, angel on my right. If you are to court the unknown, if you are to attempt to tame elephants, be prepared for a similar eventuality. If you are able, embrace it, for it is a sure sign of the undertaking's credibility. Too often, we retreat. All too commonplace are phrases like "If I had only done this when I had the chance," or "I'm not a runner, I couldn't do that," or "Who starts a business at my age?" We are so quick to encourage the dreamers in our lives, but we are so slow to embrace the dreamer within. Fear, trepidation, a suddenly elevated heart rate: all are signs that we are taking on a worthy challenge. Do not be frightened into inaction. It is the mission of the angel on your right shoulder to cheer you on and see you through. The devil on the left seeks to derail you and eliminate your momentum, knowing that once you gather momentum, much like a snowball headed down the mountain, you eventually will become an unstoppable force.

Those that have accomplished much are of no more talent than you or me; they simply have become better at recognizing all of these things and moving through them quicker and more proficiently with each success. No one is immune from fear or doubt; some are just better at dealing with it. I was a rookie, and this race was a big stretch. Staring at the acceptance email in front of me, I was struggling with the devil's incessant chant of, "Now what the hell are you gonna do, Mr. Big-Time Wannabe Adventurer?"

There is an old story that I remember only the gist of, but the message is what's really important. An invading conqueror, upon reaching the shore and unloading all his forces, ordered his ship to sail away, giving strict orders not to return. His troops, dismayed and confused at their only means of safety now gone, inquired of the captain what he had done.

"It is quite simple. We win or we die. There will be no retreat." The story continues that given no easy way out, outnumbered, on foreign ground, and unsure of what lay ahead, the troops' victory was assured because they had neither the option of retreat nor failure.

While filling out my application weeks prior and reading the race description, feelings of doubt had nagged me, but filling in my credit card info and hitting "submit" was my version of the captain sending the boat away. If the race director deemed me worthy and accepted my application, then I was committed. No retreat.

I love this quote by Kenneth Blanchard: "There's a difference between interest and commitment. When you're interested in doing something, you do it only when it's convenient. When you're committed to something, you accept no excuses; only results." I am sure that many before me and countless others after have visited the Yukon River Quest website, interested in the information and stories found there. I was not interested; I was committed, devil on my left shoulder be damned. Yukon, here I come.

Chapter 10

I WAS WELL OVER MY SKIS ON THIS ONE. IT FELT AS IF AT ANY moment, this big swing could result in a monumental pile up. The distance from Whitehorse to Dawson City, Yukon, was 715 kilometers. My longest paddle to date? Perhaps fifty miles. Unknowingly, I had enlisted the assistance of the heavens. Rules of the universe, of which I was then just vaguely aware, were now being put to the test.

Now, some twelve years later as I write this, I can attest to a simple truth: the universe supports those who dare. It doesn't matter whether or not you're qualified to take on the test. Nobel Peace Prize laureate Ellen Johnson Sirleaf exhorts, "The size of your dreams must always exceed your current capacity to achieve them." I suggest, as the quote confirms, that if we are already qualified for the dream, it's not much of a dream in the first place. I like imagining the secretary to the universe as they look over the constant stream of dreams passing by, occasionally exclaiming "Yes! Finally, something worthy of our powers. Get Luck, Fate, and Coincidence on the line; we have a real kindred spirit here to help!"

The point is that we are capable of so much more than we imagine. We can see looking back that most dreams, once accomplished, were only a small test of what we can achieve. The beauty, however, is that with each accomplishment we gain confidence in the universal laws and begin to trust that we are only limited by our own imagination.

The universe delights in the endless possibility of all things. Armed with the knowledge that "impossible" exists only within our own minds, the world becomes our playground.

If you knew without exception that failure was not an option, would the size and scope of your dreams change?

Chapter 11

How in the hell would I even train for this thing?

It wasn't as if I had never paddled before, but 715 kilometers? Come on. The race FAQ let all racers know that Carmacks, the first and (at the time) only mandatory checkpoint, was a bit over halfway at just 400 kilometers downriver. (A second three-hour rest stop now exists downriver from Carmacks at Coffee Creek Kaminak camp.) All racers, regardless of skill or pace, were required to check in and rest at Carmacks before paddling on. Well, that certainly was a relief! Just 400 kilometers. Only 300 kilometers farther than I had ever paddled at once. Cue the sweaty armpits. Shit, what had I gotten myself into? The FAQ page initially filled me with wonder and excitement. Now, the words "mosquito," "hypothermia," and "grizzly" were not so inviting. Suddenly I understood the lyrics, "Everyone wants to go to heaven, but nobody wants to die."

Maybe I should have just chalked this one up to hubris and bravado, kept my mouth shut, and forgotten about this foolishness. No one would be the wiser were I to simply not show up. Well, the race directors would, marking me a DNS ("did not start") on race day in the Yukon, but who cares? I didn't even know where the damn place was yet.

The doubts coming rapid-fire sought only to keep me safe, but safety was not what I yearned for. Adventure—losing what was false and discovering what was real for me—was the course I was now set on. Race information warned of many dangers, but it also shared advice on how to best mitigate those dangers. The winds of Lake Laberge, the most dangerous portion of the course, could blow in suddenly from the south, creating swells that challenged even the best of paddlers. Lose it here, and a cold swim would greet you. For an idea of what it's like, I dare you to head to your tub, turn the water on as cold as it gets, dump in a few bags of ice, and hop in. Welcome to the Yukon River.

Grizzly bears outnumber humans in this area. The chances of seeing one are remote, but if a meeting does occur, the consequences are, at best, soiling yourself. Class II rapids in a couple of sections? No big deal until it's actually you in the boat. Not every challenge had a solution offered by the race directors. In some cases, they gave just a bit of guidance, perhaps a thought or two, but mostly they said you'd have to figure out what works for you.

My mind focused on a quotation by André Gide. "It is only in adventure that some people succeed in knowing themselves—in finding themselves." Years prior, sitting in a jail cell serving a seven-day sentence for my second drunk driving arrest, I had set out on my first and most important adventure—getting sober. The goal had been no different then than it was now: I wanted to find myself. The Yukon River Quest, though deserving of my utmost respect, paled in comparison to that enormous undertaking so many years ago. I was reminded that "one step, one hour, one day at a time—anything is possible." I got through many days by telling myself, "Tomorrow, I may get as drunk as a sailor, but not today. Not today."

Tomorrow, I may decide to say "Screw this race," but not today. Today, I'd do a bit more research on how best to handle a potential run-in with a grizzly bear. I was back on course. Thanks, André.

Chapter 12

"IF YOU TIP YOUR KAYAK AND DON'T KNOW HOW TO PROPERLY release your spray skirt, you'll never get out. You'll drown underneath your boat."

OK, the instructor had my full attention.

Paddling for me, be it in adventure races or in training runs down our local rivers, had been in canoes or in my kayak. The nature of those waters, fairly calm and without much current, made a spray skirt unnecessary. For those wondering what the hell a spray skirt is, it's much like a skirt in that you slip it on in the same manner. Although my skirt-wearing has not been extensive, I believe it's done by putting both legs in and shimmying your way into it, depending on the tightness of said skirt, until it's up around your waist.

The spray skirt, however, still requires clothing below, as it does not drape down around the legs. It rests snugly around the hips, extending horizontally a foot or two front and back, and is made of a rubbery membrane material. You slip into your kayak and then attach the skirt firmly around the lip of the cockpit, sealing the water out and yourself in.

"Once you tip your kayak—and if you kayak long enough, you surely will—the spray skirt will be pressurized by the water. It don't matter how strong you are, it ain't coming off unless you keep your cool and do it right."

Yes, I was still paying attention. I got it. You tip over, you freak out, you die.

This was not a natural thing for me to do, going to a class. I had always been more of a "by the seat of my pants" type. My mantra was, "I'll figure it out as I go." No better way to learn than to do.

* * *

My parents divorced when I was young. My sophomore year, Mom remarried a dentist from Mediapolis, Iowa. That was just twelve miles up the road from Burlington, but it may as well have been another planet. Burlington was the big city—35,000 people—and Mediapolis was the sticks, as far as I was concerned. Farming community, pickup trucks, and country music. I hated it, and it was not so fond of me either. Today, it's one of my favorite places on Earth, though it hasn't changed one bit.

My stepfather's name is Brad Bork, and I am thankful to him in more ways than I will ever be able to tell him. A true renaissance man, he could seemingly do anything he set his mind to. I'm not just talking about teaching himself how to use a chainsaw or changing the oil in his car. He rebuilt a 1969 GTO—and I mean all of it. He designed and built the most beautiful furniture: amazing rolltop desks, grandfather clocks, and more. How did he do this all as a dentist? He just did. I can only imagine it came from his upbringing as a rancher's kid in South Dakota. You learned by doing.

I was just a punk kid going nowhere and raging against all that I could. Mad at the world for my parents' divorce, I didn't give a damn about anything, but he helped turn me around.

Sneaking in the back door was no easy task. Jingle bells were hung on it to alert Brad and Mom to my entry. It was nearly three in the morning, I was a sophomore in high school, and I was drunk. If I got caught, there would be a steep price to pay. Slowly turning the handle…slowly…slowly…a barely perceptible creak, but not so much as the slightest jingle. I got a few steps in, closing the door slowly…slowly…a little creak…and there, the door was closed. I was in. Heading for the basement where I often slept, I was home free.

"WHAT THE HELL DO YOU THINK YOU'RE DOING?!"

I nearly pooped my pants right there on the spot. Somewhere close by, shrouded in darkness, Brad had been waiting for me. Knowing him as I do, I often think of him with a wry grin on his face. There was no grin then, however, and what happened next, even in my altered state, stuck with me forever.

The booming shout was for effect. Much like the dire warnings from my paddling teacher later in life, he had my full attention. Now began the lesson.

"If you're gonna live in this house, there's gonna be some rules, son."

I thought, *Here we go. I've heard this before, 'My way or the highway,' right? Rules, rules, rules…blah blah blah.*

"I don't care how late you want to stay out."

What? Perhaps I was more drunk than I thought, though that was hard to imagine.

"You can come home any damn time you please, it's your choice. You get home at eleven, you're all good. Twelve, I'll be getting you up at six. One? I'll be getting you up at five. Two? Then it's four. And if you pull this 3:00 a.m. again, don't bother going to sleep. Good night, son."

Sitting on the couch in the basement, I pondered what just happened. I couldn't wrap my head around it. You mean it's my choice? I'm not grounded, no "you gotta learn about the real world" speech? I would later test his resolve. Cutting firewood at

5:00 a.m. sealed the lesson. I was far from perfect after that, but he had planted a seed of self-responsibility that still grows today.

Years later, a friend and I had a need for some very specialized bike racks. This was after Brad had perfected his welding skills, but that's another story for another time (I'm telling you, the guy is a self-taught genius). Team Bad Boy consisted of a 100-quart cooler, a full wet bar, a fifty-five-gallon steel drum "smoker," and after years of hearing, "You guys have everything but the kitchen sink," a kitchen sink. All of these were mounted on bicycles. Countless aluminum racks had been put to the test, all failing throughout the years. Brad was all too excited to take on the challenge. Angles, weight loads, steel, and welding? You may as well have been lowering a carcass into a pool of piranhas.

"Soon as you boys wanna drive down here, I'll be ready."

Mike (cooler guy) and I (cooker guy) headed south from Iowa City, bikes in tow. Brad met us at his garage. You would have thought it was Christmas or something. He was so excited. I'd long ago begun enjoying his childlike sense of wonder and excitement in a new challenge. Steel-cutting ensued, mad scientist-type pencil drawings on the benches. He'd cut a couple pieces of steel, and then it was "OK, cut these next eight pieces to this size, and I'll be back in fifteen minutes to check on you two." And he left.

Really? Mike and I just looked at each other, shrugging, and got to work. No better way than by doing it, I guess. We goofed a bit, wasted a piece or two, but upon his return the pieces were cut, and feeling pretty full of ourselves, we gave him the "What do you think of that?" look. He loved it. The teacher was teaching, not lecturing. Much like that late night so many years prior, you learned from being given the keys, so to speak. I thought to myself, *Give a man a fish, and you feed him for a day. Teach a man to fish and you feed him for a lifetime.*

He gave us both welding masks. He didn't use one, since he was so skilled that he could lay down a line without needing to actually look at it. He handed the torch to Mike and let him have a go. Once he was sufficiently comfortable that we wouldn't burn anything down or blow anything up, he left us again.

"Weld this to this and that to that, and I'll be back to check on you in an hour or so."

They may not be the prettiest things, but those racks have taken that cooler and grill over the Rocky Mountains, up Mount Evans (over 14,000 feet), on numerous Ride the Rockies tours, and through nearly twenty Register's Annual Great Bike Ride Across Iowa.

These lessons have served me well: don't shirk a challenge just because you don't know everything about it. Learn as much as you can, be it through research, practice, or ideally both.

Back in the kayaking class, I walked into the chilly waters, spray skirt snugly around my hips, and stepped into the cockpit. First leg, second leg, ease onto the seat. Slide the paddle underneath the kayak's bungee-like cords so as not to lose it in the water. I began stretching the spray skirt over the lip of the cockpit, creating an airtight seal that would someday keep the frigid waters of the Yukon where they belonged: out of the boat. It was a slightly claustrophobic sensation. The kayak and I were now attached. It was equal parts cool and scary, this new piece of equipment. Tip over, lose your cool, and you will drown. I was reminded of the earlier warnings, which felt much more real now that I was sealed in this damn thing.

"All right, when you're ready, flip yourself upside down in your boat."

It's one thing to see it done and totally another to be the "flippee." I was reminded of Brad's lessons, years earlier. This was no different. Self-rescue, self-responsibility. You're the boss of your own destiny, he had taught me. He would teach me enough to be dangerous and then let me learn by the best of all ways, doing.

I took a few deep breaths, rocked the boat, and upside down I went. Into the unknown.

Chapter 13

THE TOWN HAD TWO STOP SIGNS. ONE WAS ON THE CORNER, BUR-
ied deep into the ground. The other was on wheels, sitting in
the middle of the busiest intersection in town. Mediapolis,
Iowa—population 1,553 according to the 2016 Census—was
known statewide as a "little engine that could" for its six-on-six
girls' basketball powerhouse. Among high school sports fans, it
was known nationwide. Iowa was at that time, I believe, the last
remaining state playing six-on-six ball. As a boys' basketball player
at the age of sixteen, though, this was more a source of jealousy
than pride.

If you aren't familiar, here it is in a nutshell: on one half of the
court, you had three girls on offense, and on the other you had
three on defense. If you scored, the ref grabbed the ball as it exited
the net and threw it to half-court, where it was then handed off to
the offensive team on that side, who then gave it their best shot.
Sounds archaic, right? To me, much of the place I called home as
a teenager seemed out of date. Though it was only twelve miles
north of "the big city" of Burlington, it was like I had somehow
entered a new reality or some sort of time warp.

The trophy cases were filled with evidence of the program's
excellence dating back decades. The Bullettes were coached by
an extraordinary man who touched, taught, and inspired all who
came to know him. The word "legend" can be used a bit loosely,
but in the case of Vernon "Bud" McLearn, it is perhaps an under-
statement. It is my hope that you have the pleasure of meeting a

person or two who are of similar ilk. Born in 1933, he coached from 1959 to 1987. Bud McLearn did more than coach, however; he was a teacher, a leader, and a molder of people, and not just the young ladies he coached.

If I had a talent in any academic arena, it was numbers. I could eat up hours giving myself miniature math tests during family road trips. "Six times six...thirty-six. Square root of eighty-one is nine. What numbers cannot be divided by any other number other than one and themselves? Two, three, five, seven, eleven, thirteen, seventeen, nineteen, twenty-three...And what if I multiplied them? Five times seven? Thirty-five. Eleven times thirteen? 143. Seventeen times nineteen? 323." I am much slower now, but the mental exercise even as I write these words still brings me joy.

Like so much else in my life at the time, I chose to dislike everything—even the things I liked. The wounds from my parents' divorce were still open after many years, and I attempted to fill them with poor choices and refusing to care about anything, even something as safe and unthreatening as numbers.

Why Bud ever took notice of me I'll never know. I was shooting jump shots, working on my game alone before practice, when he appeared a bit out of nowhere. He unassumingly said, "Hi," introduced himself, and began breaking down the science and form of the jump shot. He did so with a wit and caring that made it easy to forget you were sharing space with "the man." Despite my jealousy of the girls' success, even an outsider like me knew Coach McLearn's reputation. I would have never had the stones to approach him, and he really had no reason to approach me. Or did he? Was this man more than just a coach?

Only the fear of losing my basketball privileges had kept my algebra grades above a D my junior year. It just so happened that the teacher was also my basketball coach, and we were like oil and water. This was much more due to me than him, a fact that I would not realize until many years later.

Coach McLearn taught an advanced mathematics class for those seniors who excelled in the numbers. Our first "jump shot clinic"—I doubt his real intention was to make me a better shot, although he surely would derive joy from improvement in that as well—had provided me access. I felt comfortable with the man, and somehow he saw behind my walls and lured out the kid who delighted in number puzzles and brainteasers. He allowed me entry into the advanced class. Almost every class session began with a problem, a puzzle, a lesson to be worked on, pondered, researched, and brought back in later days. The school year was made up of four quarters. The first quarter I earned an A- in math. It would be the worst mark I'd receive in his class that year. I can say without question that in the entirety of my formative years, I only found joy in his course.

Coach McLearn was a teacher not of math or of basketball, but of life. He reveled in the pursuit of excellence. He expected and saw the best that we could be, regardless of where we came from. He saw an opportunity for excellence in us all.

His accomplishments in the classroom and in life are immeasurable. His accomplishments on the court, however, *are* measurable. His Wikipedia page spells some of them out:

During his 26-year tenure at Mediapolis, the girls' team went 333-8 (97.6 percent) on their home court. This run included consecutive home winning streaks of 97, 84, and 66 games. McLearn's teams qualified for the Iowa state tournament 21 years out of the 28 (including a stretch of 12-straight appearances), with two state championships, a 51–35 victory over South Hamilton (Hamilton County) in

1967 and a 68–51 win over Adel in 1973. He retired in 1987 with the fourth best record in Iowa state basketball history. McLearn and Mediapolis lost to Van Horne High School, 62–59, in the 1962 state tournament final (Van Horne's Mickey Schallau scored 37 of the team's 62 points).

McLearn was inducted into the Iowa Girls Coaches Association Hall of Fame in 1988, and after dying of cancer in 1999, was posthumously inducted into the National High School Athletic Coaches Association Hall of Fame in 2000. The high school gymnasium at Mediapolis was named McLearn Court in his honor in 2001.

It should be noted that Coach McLearn's teams did all this at a time when there were no "classes" for girls' basketball in the state of Iowa. That's right—to get to those twenty-one of twenty-eight, including twelve straight state tournaments, they had to beat every big school in the state, some with enrollments bigger than our entire town.

At the intersection of Highway 61 and Yarmouth Road is my hometown. Were it not for the speed limit signs that slow you to thirty-five miles per hour or so, you could easily miss it. Mediapolis, Iowa: where I learned that big dreams can launch from anywhere. They are not a product of what is outside of you, not determined by the size of the town you call home, your economic background, or your ethnicity. City boy, farm kid, black, white, short, tall, male, or female; believe you can, and you can. Celebrate your mentors, thank them, and continue their legacy by doing the same for someone else. Our life is our message.

Could a kid from Mediapolis really take on the world's longest kayak race? Is it possible that we can be whoever and whatever we aspire to be? Could one of the smallest little towns in Iowa dominate girls' basketball for nearly three decades? Vernon "Bud" McLearn taught so many of us the answer to these questions is a resounding yes.

Chapter 14

TWO THOUSAND, ONE HUNDRED AND SIXTY-NINE MILES FROM Des Moines, Iowa, to Whitehorse, Yukon Territory, Canada. Even now, "thumbing" out those words—I write my books on my iPhone—as I sit here in my hometown coffeeshop, Mars Cafe, it brings goose bumps and amazement remembering the journey.

Paddling sessions provided the opportunity to hone my skills, build endurance, and reflect. Guiding my kayak under the highway bridge, the sound of car after pickup truck after semi rolling by overhead interrupted my communion with the gently flowing waters below. Pausing the paddle, I glanced quickly at my watch—which went mostly unnoticed, as time holds little meaning in the wild places—and realized it was nearly 5:00 p.m. Folks were headed home from work. I imagined at about this same time every Monday through Friday, you could find them here.

I wondered if they ever glanced left or right crossing the bridge. Did they hear the river's invitation? Just for a moment, were they able to take in its beauty—a beauty they were a part of? Or did it go unnoticed, obscured by the chatter of the mind? I wondered how many times I've ignored the beauty right next to me?

Only recently have I taken the time to really look at the majestic oak in my front lawn. It towers above my home. For how many decades—heck, maybe centuries, for all I know—has it done so? All along it has been there; it was I who was not. Yes, I existed, but I was so busy in my day-to-day routines that the tree stood there unnoticed. I'm working on slowing down. It is amazing the simple beauties surrounding us all, if we just take a second and look around.

How is this my life? I asked myself, traffic buzzing by overhead. How am I so lucky to be here on this river? This river where my only traffic concern is the occasional deadfall tree that has lost its battle with time or erosion, beginning a new journey downstream, eventually returning to the earth. This was not to compare or to suggest that somehow my life was of any higher quality than those who passed overhead, but I guessed that given the opportunity, at least a few would excitedly change places at that moment.

I was reminded of a quote from "the spiritually incorrect mystic," Osho: "I have meditated in both an ox cart and a Rolls Royce. The Rolls Royce was better." Which is to say that those on life's highway above could be every bit as happy and content at that moment as I, perhaps even more so. Given the choice, though—and we all are—I'll take the river rush hour every time.

The race and its 700-plus kilometers en route to Dawson City would present its own unique challenges. First things first, though. *How the heck do I even get to the Yukon? Shit, that's a really good question.* By good, I meant it passed the litmus test of any real question, which is that the initial answer is "I have no freak-ing idea." It also gained credibility as a worthy question when it spawned another: *How the hell do I get my gear there?* Which led to *What am I taking?* Followed by *My kayak, oh crap, what about my kayak?* The questions came rapid-fire.

Beware when taking on big dreams. The mind, in its effort to protect, can question you into paralysis, burying you under a mountain of unknowns. Recognize this, and all is good. These questions, mounting with each second or two, were valid. They were certainly worthy of time and attention, but I would not be taking the mind's bait. I wouldn't get caught up in the storm attempting to brew in my mind. How do you eat an elephant? One bite at a time. I placed myself safely inside the eye of the storm, taking notes on those questions that had surfaced, returning to the first, focusing my efforts on answering it, and trusting that the answers would be revealed to each subsequent one in its own time.

The Race to the Midnight Sun was officially underway.

Chapter 15

I ONCE ATTENDED A PRESENTATION AT A MULTILEVEL MARKETING conference on insurance. The company dealt with educating folks about the best way to be financially independent, which add-ons were rip-offs, what things made sense, and what things didn't. I am no fan of the dentist, apologies to my wonderful stepdad who was one. To this day, we have a running contest of who has last been to the dentist. Let's just say it's been so long neither of us know who is winning or, depending on your take on oral hygiene, losing the contest. Heading into the lecture that day, I'd equated it to going to the dentist. If it had been available, I'd have asked for a shot of Novocain to ease the pain. To my surprise, it was one of the most memorable presentations I have had the privilege to attend. The gentleman was funny and dynamic, and dare I say he made insurance fun, at least for an hour. I'm hopeful that sharing the planning and logistics with you in this chapter doesn't have you begging for a painkiller halfway through.

You can't go to Whitehorse, Yukon, from the United States without a passport, so in the spirit of "first things first," I thought, *How and where do I get a passport?* The question, by itself, was exciting to me because the only reason for me to need one was that a great adventure awaited. Perhaps it seems trivial, but it had much more importance than you might ordinarily think. It was another step in the early stages of a grand undertaking, and those early steps, seemingly trivial on their own individual merits, created momentum—and momentum is everything. Momentum feeds upon itself, spawns confidence, and eventually becomes a force that is unstoppable. At some point in this process, the mind will resist no more. Realizing you are serious, it will begin to rally fully behind you.

I smiled as big as I could.

"No smiling. They don't want folks smiling," the passport photographer admonished.

Whoever "they" were, I hoped they wouldn't be sitting next to me on the flight to Canada. I didn't give in without a fight, though. Eventually my photographer got a giggle from me trying to sneak in a smirk as she snapped each photo. You can't tell from looking at my final photo, but I am grinning inside. I'd given myself ample time for the four- to six-week processing time. If your big adventure is just a couple of weeks away and you're needing a passport fast, don't despair; they do offer an expedited service for a few bucks extra. No smiling allowed for that one either. Sorry.

If I was going to go to the Yukon, which now was pretty much a foregone conclusion, I was going to soak up as much time there as possible. It would be my goal to immerse myself in the place and engage all my senses. To visit the place—to see it, touch it, hear it, taste it—yes, that was good; but there is more available for those looking. There is a feel to it, a heartbeat, a current that runs deeper than the river that calls the place home. Generations have learned how to survive, live, and even thrive here. I longed to experience the place and let it take me in. I'd share what I could and bring back as much of it as I could hold. No way was I just gonna fly in, paddle till my arms fell off, and return home. Clearly the race was the reason I was going—or so I thought.

Chapter 16

NATALIE GOLDBERG, IN HER AMAZING BOOK *WRITING DOWN the Bones*, which is only partially a book about writing, shares this thought: "Original details are very ordinary, except to the mind that sees their extraordinariness."

One day, two people were walking to work. Each of them took the exact same walk each day, leaving their homes with just enough time to cover the distance between home and office. The walk was not far, just under a mile.

Arriving at their destinations, one headed straight away for the coffee, and heaven forbid it not be ready. That first cup held the keys to the kingdom. To start the day without it would be dire for sure. The other merrily entered their place of work with a spring in her step and a song in her heart that was perceptible to those who may be listening for such things. "Hopefully the coffee is on. If not, no biggie. I'll prepare it." She actually enjoyed the opportunity to make the coffee and occasionally showed up a bit early just to do so, knowing the jump-start it gave to those that came in looking for it.

Jim, as we'll call him, walked fifteen minutes every day to the office, his mind jumping from thought to thought. Perhaps it was focused on last night's politics or his son's trouble at school. Maybe there was a project nagging at him, a client needing this or that. *How in the heck will I make quota this month? Man, if those three new accounts don't order by Thursday…* And soon enough, it's in the door and straight for the coffee.

Jenny, as we'll call her, lived just a few blocks from Jim. On occasion they'd make their walks at about the same time, although Jenny took a different route almost every day. When on similar paths, Jenny would raise a hand and smile. Jim always seemed a bit preoccupied, and his reply seemed perfunctory.

Jenny's walk was always invigorating—extraordinary, if you will. Sure, Jim knew there were a few trees along the way, but Jenny truly saw each tree. She gave it life, and it returned life without hesitation. It was an unspoken deal, and she recognized the value of the trees. She saw their agreement as one of the many miracles on her morning walk. Each day she would take a new route, but the game was always the same. She'd leave the house excited: turning the key in the apartment door, putting a smile on her face, stepping outside, and wondering which way the wind blew today. If it was in her face, she did not rail; she welcomed it, took it in, and was grateful for it. At her back? Well, then the walk would be a bit warmer and slightly easier. That was perfect also. And so each day Jenny began her walk to work, but she didn't see it as a walk to work. She was on an adventure, led by the same question each day: *How many miracles can I experience this morning?* Two people taking similar physical journeys each morning. One person's mundane is another's miracle. How many miracles do we pass by each morning?

Until this point in my life, lists had *always* been mundane. But not this list. With each item, I chose to go deeper. Sleeping pad, check. Sleeping bag, check. Mundane. Mundane. Ah, but wait—I elected to let the list take me on an adventure. The sleeping pad was of my own making. It was nothing extraordinary, sitting there in the corner, made of two silver reflective pieces of roofing insulation folded onto each other, kind of how you would fold a piece of bread if you were making a one-slice peanut butter sandwich.

I duct-taped the seams together to ensure that water did not penetrate. Although I'm proud of the creation, its existence still probably falls short of exciting for you. The sleeping bag wasn't sexy laying on the floor among other gear. Put a checkmark by it on the list, move it to the "taking" pile on the other side of the room, and move on. Right? Usually, for me, yes. And had I done so this time, mundane would have won the day.

But I let my mind wander.

"It's been a cold, damp spring up here. You'll want to make sure you stay good and dry if you're heading out to the campground for the evening." I appreciated the advice from the barrel-chested old man at the coffeeshop that had taken the time to chat me up.

I imagined my arrival in Whitehorse.

It was a two-and-a-half-mile walk to the campground, upriver from Whitehorse. With a week of walking back and forth to town, as I had arrived plenty early, I was thankful for the lightweight nature of my sleeping pad. Each little bit took a load off my rookie backpacking legs.

Imagining the walk and all of its amazing firsts, time went quickly.

The ground was as the old man had said. Damp. Cold.

The boring old tarp, item four on the list, was laid out on the ground. As it lay in the corner of my apartment, it suddenly took on a bit more life. The tent, item seven, would sit upon it for the week, nice and dry, providing a second layer of insulation.

I rolled out the sleeping pad, taking just a moment to lie down, dry, insulated and comfortable, closing my eyes for just a moment to listen to the sounds of the Yukon for the very first time.

This was not just a list I was writing; it was a dress rehearsal, a preview of what could be. What could have been simply words on paper had been transformed into my first journey to the

Yukon Territory. There was no way of knowing if the sounds I heard while picturing it all were accurate; it didn't matter. I decided to stay a bit longer.

I rolled out item two from the list, my sleeping bag, laid it on top of item one, my sleeping pad, and let all of the great unknown rock me to sleep.

List-making like this can be exhausting. Items eight through fourteen would have to wait.

Lists. Mundane versus miraculous. We all have a choice.

Chapter 17

IT RESEMBLED A GARAGE SALE, BUT IT WAS SO MUCH MORE. THE living room of my one-bedroom apartment in the center of Des Moines had a small path that allowed for travel from the bedroom to the back—and only—door, which stood just past the kitchen. Gear took up the remaining available space. It wasn't lost on me that pretty much all of it (minus the backpack) would be in or on my kayak. I laughed, sort of, as I remembered The Beverly Hillbillies with all their possessions piled high on their pickup truck or the Grinch making a dash out of Whoville with all the Christmas gifts overloading his sled.

On my longest training paddles, I took some of this stuff, but I'd never fully loaded it. This was a mistake. I've since learned the value of training like you're racing. That's not to say you have to go full "parade float" each workout, but flesh out your system: where things go, how you're going to store what, and where. What needs be most accessible if, say, you were in need of another layer? What if it began to suddenly rain? In thirty- or forty-degree weather, having to dig through seven different items before getting to your raincoat not only drenches you, it also means all the things you just pulled out are now wet.

Read through the Yukon River Quest website, and the word *hypothermia* comes up more than once. One small detail like packing a raincoat can mean the difference between paddling nice and cozy, just a few rain drops finding their way to you, and being teeth-chatteringly damp for an entire evening. These lessons are often learned the hard way. Trust me, ten miles from home and a warm fire while training was a far better place to learn a lesson than 100 kilometers from anywhere in the middle of the Yukon bush. I'd packed as thoroughly as I knew how, bringing my sleeping bag, pad, small stove, small gas canisters, and a couple of lights.

Clothing obviously was my top concern. In any type of endurance racing, but especially in places where cold or wet could be an issue, regulating your body heat is *huge*. Sweat is the enemy. It's nearly unavoidable but usually manageable. Light, wicking (keeps the moisture off your skin) underlayers with zippers so you can start to ventilate once the body's warm are a necessity. Cotton in any form is a no-no. Once wet, it stays wet. Keep your head warm. Pack a couple of beanies to wear while racing, maybe a nice bulky stocking cap for hanging out at a checkpoint or catching some sleep, and make sure your jackets have hoods. I'd packed a few pairs of neoprene waterproof socks and gloves also. Cold extremities suck. I don't care if it's a trail run, a fat bike ride in the snow, or being on a beach when the sun goes down; if your hands, feet, or head are cold, you're miserable. It makes no difference how warm your core is, cold extremities will suck the fun right out of you.

I still wasn't sure how the food was going to play out. Winning or fast solo kayak times for the race were in the sixty-hour range. I had no misconceptions about challenging that. The longest race in hours for me up to that time was thirty-six. Potentially, I could be looking at seventy-five hours or more. Unfortunately, there weren't many riverside convenience stores along the route. None, to be exact. We would be able to have a drop bag waiting down river, but I was unsure about how I would handle my nutrition, which was nagging me.

I had some ideas and reading race reports gave good information, but all participants did it differently. I'd have to soak up as much info as I could, combine it with past race experience, and hope for the best. There was only so much space in a kayak. What I was looking at—covering most of an entire room's floor—all needed to be on the journey with me. I wasn't sure how I'd fit it all in my backpack and on the damn plane. On top of this was the dilemma of my kayak. Shipping my girl to the Yukon would be a huge pain, logistically and financially. Not shipping her would mean taking on the Yukon River in a boat I'd be unfamiliar with. It's said that you pack all your uncertainties the first time you do a race, which is to say that you typically pack way too much shit. "Better safe than sorry" seemed prudent racing advice in an environment that could actually kill you. Hypothermia; moose, bear, and wolf attacks; drowning. All could end you. Experience teaches and refines. To really learn is to do. Ask questions, watch others, read all you can, but eventually you have to put up or shut up.

Taking one last look over my shoulder as I headed through the walking path in the living room, I realized that uncertainty was the only thing I was certain of. It was time for bed. My flight left the next morning at 7:05 a.m. I wondered if I'd be able to sleep.

Chapter 18

FIFTEEN HOURS, TWENTY-SEVEN MINUTES. DES MOINES, IOWA, to Minneapolis, Minnesota. Minneapolis on to Vancouver, British Columbia. Vancouver to Whitehorse, Yukon Territory, Canada.

"Next please. Next please…"

A tap on my right shoulder from behind brought me back to the present. I had heard the lady as she inquired nicely. I just didn't "hear" her. My mind had been somewhere else—somewhere between my hometown and the place I would soon call home for the next twelve days. The backpack, which was heavier than I remembered, and I stepped forward, heeding the airline assistant's call.

"Wow, the Yukon, huh? That sounds like quite an adventure." She accepted my passport, which I was using for identification purposes for the first time.

This would be a trip of many firsts. Some were known, but how many were unknown? Well…I didn't know. I made myself a quick promise, silently: *No matter how many times I am fortunate to use this passport, I promise to treat each time with wonder, excitement, and thanks.*

While tagging my baggage, which I was all too happy to get off my shoulders, she inquired, "Why are you going up there?"

"The world's longest kayak race is there." It was the primary reason for the trip, but I could have issued many additional answers as well: to see one of the last frontiers, one of a few places still mostly untouched by human beings. Whitehorse is the largest city in the Yukon Territory. It is also the only city. It is a land where moose outnumber humans.

Three years before, I had answered a starving soul's call for what I would label my first big adventure.

Big is such a difficult word, and it is inherently dangerous because it invites comparison. I could easily argue that the biggest and most profound adventure of my life had been getting sober so I didn't spend the rest of my life in jail or end up dead. Or perhaps it had been my first 5K, which led me far beyond my imagination, eventually running around the entirety of Lake Michigan. So "big" is different to us all. Your "big" is yours and no one else's. Be proud of it. In any case, three years earlier, I had loaded my bicycle, pedaled west from my apartment, and eventually hopped on the bike trail out of town. I had been headed west. That's all. Just west.

At the age of twenty-four, Alastair Humphreys left his home in England. Sixty countries, five continents, four years, and 46,000 miles later, he had circled the world. He was quoted as saying, "It's a great thing. The sidewalk outside your door can take you completely around the world."

My journey eventually took me through western Iowa, Nebraska, the Badlands of South Dakota, Wyoming, and down into Colorado. Two thousand miles, forty-nine days, twelve mountain passes, and one trail marathon. The sidewalk outside my door led me beyond just miles of endless adventure; it awakened me.

"To test myself, physically and mentally," I could have continued with my reply to her question of "Why?"

These self-imposed challenges gave purpose to my existence. Since my parents' divorce, I had always raged against my father when he told me, "Someday, son, you're going to have to get with the program." Then it was just a rage against my pain. It had since spawned deeper thoughts, however.

Why are we here? Who am I? Who can I be? What do I want my journey to look like? When the lights go out, will I grip tightly, hoping to get even one more breath, or will I happily acquiesce—knowing I had drunk fully and been true to myself—give thanks, and go smiling, excited for the next adventure that lay in wait…beyond?

Her look indicated she would have enjoyed the time to hear such thoughts. Perhaps just that initial answer had been enough to awaken her spirit. Perhaps it would be enough that she'd head home after work and remember the tall bearded fellow, bright-eyed and headed off to the Yukon. Maybe, just maybe, she would decide she had put off her big adventure long enough. I liked that thought.

"Gate C, flight to Minneapolis-St. Paul will begin boarding shortly."

Chapter 19

I was Lieutenant John J. Dunbar from *Dances with Wolves*, headed to see, feel, and become the frontier, before it was gone forever. Or perhaps I was Denys Finch Hatton, a man who refused to be tamed in the classic book *Out of Africa*. Setting my sails with only the known behind and the horizon ahead, I was Earnest Shackleton. Wide-eyed and admittedly a bit scared, I walked down the jetway, leaving the safety of the terminal; the city I called home would soon be below me and many miles in the rearview.

Lowering my head slightly and entering the plane, a sense of accomplishment fell over me. Many steps had led to this one step. This step, right foot over the threshold, a sliver of an opening underfoot allowing me to glimpse the tarmac. Left foot now, and with that step I was onboard Flight 1628 to Minneapolis-St. Paul. Each step had its place, its importance. There was a unique energy with these last two steps, though.

A reality hit me at that moment. I had felt it a few times prior in my life. There was a bit of familiarity to it. *Would I be able to clean up the mess of my life?* I wondered this as I took the first steps outside the Johnson County jail, having just spent seven days in jail for my second drunk driving offense. *Could I actually run a 5K?* I questioned, finding myself on the starting line of the Saint Patrick's Day 5K in Manitou Springs, not having run so much as ten feet in probably a decade. The Garden of the Gods 10-Miler. My first marathon. Turning the first pedal stroke, not knowing where my head would rest that night, knowing only for certain of my direction—west. All of these events shared some common traits: fear, excitement, a willingness to try, a belief that I *could*, even though I never had. Each event also built on the prior one, giving birth to the knowledge that I can if I believe I can. I belong where I say I belong.

The universe supports those who dare.

Armed with this knowledge did not make me fearless; truth be told, part of me was scared shitless about what lay ahead, but a bigger part—a just slightly bigger part—reminded me to just keep moving.

I was not much for chit-chat on planes. I wasn't much for chit-chat anywhere, really. That is changing slowly for me now, as I open up more to folks and become curious as to their lives and adventures and what they may have to teach. But then, completely immersed in my own adventure, the plane may as well have been empty.

Does taking off in an airplane make you a bit scared? It does me. I'm a huge Tom Hanks fan. In *Bridge of Spies*, the Russian he defends has a calmness about him that Hanks's character finds perplexing. After all, he could be facing the death penalty. Often times, throughout the movie, Hanks asks, "Aren't you the least bit worried?" To this, the endearing older man replies, calm as can be, "Would it help?" Eventually it almost becomes a joke between the two. I have become more this way about flying, and in many respects, about worrying as a whole. Faced with things beyond my control, like taking off in a plane, I try to remind myself, "Will worrying help?" The answer is always the same—and it's comforting. Then and still now, though a bit less, I hold on tightly during take off. It doesn't help.

The wheels were up. Out my window to the left, the bike trail leading south to Cumming and further to Martensdale was visible.

The Des Moines skyline stood proudly out the windows to the right. Slowly, wisps of clouds began to interrupt the view until the plane was fully submerged, and the city disappeared. The slight turbulence subsided as the plane pulled itself through the clouds. A bright blue sky welcomed us; a calm settled. The Twin Cities were just an hour or so away, and then it would be on to Vancouver. Mesmerized by the endless mountains of white, fluffy clouds, so brightly illuminated by the sun, I wondered—like so many years prior, biking west—where I might lay my head for the evening in Vancouver. Planning such a thing had seemed like it would lessen the adventure. Once on the ground and through customs, I'd get my backpack, start walking, find a cab, and have it drop me in the center of the city. Just me and my overstuffed backpack. The flight to Whitehorse would not be departing until the next morning. There was much to explore before then.

Chapter 20

IS THERE AN ADVENTURE THAT WAITS FOR YOU? DO YOU DREAM of riding your bike through the California wine country, kicking off your bike shoes to stomp grapes, squishing them between your toes? Perhaps you have always dreamed of starting a business, writing a book, or taking surfing lessons and catching a wave, if only for a second. Does zip-lining the canopy of the rain forest haunt you, in a good way? Imagine it: flying like Superman at twenty or thirty miles an hour, nearly choking on the excitement, through the lushest area on the planet. I don't care if that hasn't been a dream, there's no denying that it would be remarkable.

For just a moment, right now, take a few deep breaths. Center yourself. Now, go to the place where that one dream, that unique dream, has already been accomplished. See yourself in that space. You have done it! Close your eyes for a moment and just sit in that place. Feel it fully, in every way possible. Feel how amazing that place is. Feel it, see it, touch it, smell it—dance in it! I am serious. The next sentences you'll be reading can wait. Go there; the longer the better. Deep breaths. Eyes closed. When you return, then you can continue reading.

Enjoy!

Now go to your very last moment. The one when your remaining breaths are few. It's just you now. Only you. All those around, perhaps at your bedside, are no longer in your conscious space. Time slows, and perhaps it no longer even exists. Do not move on quickly from that last sentence. This time grows closer every moment for us all.

We all have an expiration date. Day-to-day concerns, "life" and all its business, can distract us. It becomes so easy to put off our dreams until tomorrow. Someday, guaranteed, there won't be a tomorrow. Someday, you may have waited on tomorrow for so long, that with still many tomorrows waiting, you then say, "It's too late now." When those last moments come, regret will be your partner.

What if you choose to act on your dreams? Imagine those last moments. You have walked barefoot in the grass, danced in the rain, started the business, written the book, face-planted in the foamy Costa Rican waves. You have hugged all your family and most of your friends (some just wig out, but that's OK). You have soaked in the sunrise, said hello to the sun, and then at the end of the day as it set, said, *Thank you, I'll see you tomorrow if I'm lucky, and if not, I know that today I honored myself and lived to the fullest.* Like a lioness, you stalked life, paying attention to every detail possible, always ready to pounce. Death is imminent as you lie there. There is no fear, however, only excitement as you welcome the next great adventure, the ultimate unknown, knowing that you lived this adventure fully.

My life was slowly taking on this timbre. I have often wondered, "If your life was a movie, would anyone pay to see it?" There was so much more waiting for me in this life. I could feel it. I had answered my own call.

Often I asked myself, *What if this is it? What if today is the last day? Have I repaid the debt? Have I honored the gift of this one life by living it? If the lights go out tonight, will I say thank you and excitedly step into the darkness?* The answer still came with qualifications. *Yes, but now knowing my path, I hope I'm given as much time to walk it as possible.* It's so much damn fun when you know your path and, most importantly, start walking it. Hell, you might even go all Dorothy from *The Wizard of Oz* and dance down that yellow brick road. I hope you do.

I was "off to see the Wizard, the wonderful Wizard of Oz." Off the plane, never-before-stamped passport in hand, I just needed to get through customs.

A new country—Vancouver, Canada, and the Yukon Territory—lay waiting on the other side.

Chapter 21

"Good day, Mr. Cannon. Your reason for entering Canada?" the customs agent asked.

"Headed to the Yukon," I replied, a bit full of my adventurous self. "Taking on the world's longest kayak race."

I can only hazard a guess, as this was my first attempt to pass into another country, but my sense was that most answers were one word, maybe two, and the agent would manufacture a smile, stamp the passport, and grant access. Perhaps he may even follow up with an "Enjoy your stay." My instincts reckoned that with hundreds or even thousands of reasons for entering and an equal number of passports to be stamped, he had little interest or time for banter.

I could almost see it happen. Just as the words "enjoy your stay" were traveling from mind to mouth, elbow at the ready, passport about to be stamped, the gentleman caught himself.

"What's that you say? Kayak race? World's longest?"

Again, I was only guessing, but this guy snapping out of his routine was probably a rarer occurrence. The token response of "business" or "pleasure" surely was met with only a stamp of the passport and a "Next, please."

"Yep, that's right," I replied, glancing quickly over my shoulder at the hundred or more folks in line. "Off to Whitehorse. Seven hundred kilometers down the Yukon River, Whitehorse to Dawson City."

Perhaps I touched something in the man. Was he more than he appeared? Most people are. Maybe he was a great adventurer, or maybe a flicker of wanderlust burned inside of him. A few seconds' delay at customs, I surmised, was equal to minutes in other situations. This line seldom, if at all, stopped or slowed for more than the required time needed to move us travelers through.

Stamp-holding arm half-cocked, the gentleman's head raised as I replied. The man took just a moment to fully absorb my answer. With a genuine smile, he seemed to stamp my passport with not just the seal of Canada but with his own seal of approval as well.

"Good luck, man. Welcome to Canada!"

And with that, I left the United States behind for the first time in my life.

The significance of this transition struck me. Pausing a moment, I realized every step forward for nearly the next two weeks would be a new adventure. With only one deadline looming—I needed to be back in this airport tomorrow morning—time was on my side. Deciding to not waste the opportunity, my left foot took a step, and my right followed, both stopping side by side. Making sure I was as present as possible, I celebrated that moment. That one step was significant. I'd just taken a step I'd never taken before. Would it be an overstatement to say it was my own "one small step for man, one giant leap for mankind" moment? Of course it would. After all, I wasn't the first to take that step just past Customs. It was, however, a new leap for me. Never before had I been to this place. Right there, right then, I was totally present. It would be the mantra for the journey. I did not want to walk aimlessly through the airport. Human sponge mode activated. *Soak it all in, man!* I reminded myself. *Every bit of it.*

There was one last piece of the puzzle. It didn't take long till the conveyor kicked out my purple Gregory backpack. With that slung over my left shoulder, I was good to go. I'd never stayed in a hostel before. I thought that would be cool, and I hoped I could find one.

The rotating glass doors kicked me out curbside. A brisk but not overly chilly breeze met me, and I breathed in deeply. My first taste of Canadian air was sweet as any treat could have been. With nowhere to be and all day to get there, I just stood, senses alert, breathing in, listening to the sounds of Vancouver and the sounds behind the sounds. Like a symphony, every place has an aural landscape, but the overall sound is made up of so many mini-sounds. There is a depth to the symphony. Take a moment and listen, deeply. You will hear the timpani as it slowly rumbles in the background. The flute and the oboe, nearly imperceptible at times, are nevertheless so much a part of the overall sound. Cities are no different. Even where you sit at this very moment, there is a depth that perhaps you are unaware of, but close your eyes and take it in. You'll be amazed at how much is going on. The most beautiful symphony on earth, the "silence" of the wild places, waited for me in Whitehorse just a day from now.

Flagging down a cab, a conversation like the one I shared with the customs agent—albeit with more depth, as there were not hundreds of people waiting in line behind me—ensued.

"Where are you headed?"

"Downtown Vancouver, if you would."

"Anywhere in particular?"

"The middle of it."

There was a brief delay at this. "OK, you got it man. Where you heading with that backpack?"

I think you know how the rest of this conversation goes.

I asked the gentleman if he would be working in the morning, and would he mind picking me up around 7:00 a.m.? He inquired as to where, saying that he would be working, in fact.

"I can't say for sure. Somewhere within a couple miles of here."

I sensed that he liked the flying-by-the-seat-of-your-pants nature of it all. He left his card with me.

"See you in the morning."

"Sounds good. Thanks."

I'm a huge fan of Westerns; *Tombstone* is one of my favorites. In that film, upon arriving in what would be one of the last boom-towns of the West, Wyatt Earp and his brothers find themselves in front of a large window and catch their reflection. The youngest Earp, beginning to speak, is quickly cut short by his older brother Wyatt: "No, just look." He knew words would taint the moment.

Downtown Vancouver was amazingly modern, as cosmopolitan to me as I'm sure the thriving silver town of Tombstone had been to the Earps. There were giant, magnificent windows all around. Standing in the square provided endless opportunity for reflection. Backpack over both shoulders, more free than at any other time in my life, I was reminded, *No words. Just look.*

Chapter 22

IT WAS AS IF I HAD BEEN TRANSPORTED INTO THE FUTURE. I thought back to my childhood afternoons, watching *Star Trek*. "Space, the final frontier. These are the voyages of the Starship Enterprise." Occasionally, Captain James T. Kirk and the crew would beam down to an alien planet, if it was capable of supporting human life. I felt this way standing in the center of downtown Vancouver, like it was almost otherworldly. Allowing for the fact that I was a kid from small-town Iowa, take this for what you deem it's worth. If you have been to the place, my money says you were equally impressed, even if you are better travelled than I was.

For starters, the city was immaculate. Around every corner I looked quickly left or right, fully expecting to catch a glimpse of a cleaning gnome or two. I never did, but I'm certain of their existence. We're talking not so much as a stray cigarette butt or random cellophane candy wrapper. Nothing. Each window reflected quite clearly that which stood opposite. Finding even a dated building, something appearing to be built prior to, say, yesterday, presented a challenge. I'd been dropped into the middle of some cosmopolitan diorama, depicting a futuristic city sitting on an architect's conference table. Were it not for others walking around tending to their business, I might have freaked out a bit and questioned the reality of my situation. I almost felt the need to pinch myself to make sure I wasn't dreaming. With the walkabout in full swing, step one was underway. *Just walk*, I had told myself. Check. Accomplished. Stomach beginning to growl, I asked a passerby where I might find some food choices.

Kindly, the young lady pointed the way for me. "Three blocks down, hang a right, and a couple more blocks you'll look left and right, and you'll see all kinds of choices."

I *love* oysters and had been told I'd find great ones in Vancouver. It seemed like that would make a tasty after-dinner treat once my grumbling stomach was satisfied.

I walked without much of a care in the world to Carrall Street and found all sorts of retail and culinary goodness waiting just for me. In my mind, Vancouver was indeed my oyster. I'd reached that dangerous level of hungry that teeters on the brink of angry. Hangry. It's not where one wants to be, ever. Everything edible looked good. Fortunately, not far down Carrall Street, I saw Vera's Burger Shack. It was a perfectly restored two-story Victorian building with a beautiful glass storefront. An adorable caricature of an old lady donning a cow-themed chef's cap—I'm assuming it was Vera—hung over the door. It was already into the afternoon, and there was still a bit of a line. *This bodes well*, I thought. Stepping inside, I was intoxicated by the smells; my stomach ready to pounce, I grabbed a menu. Amongst the burger choices and all the different combinations of toppings, I saw "You can't beat Vera's meat" and laughed to myself. A bit of a walk would be required after throwing myself in this feedbag. Perhaps I'd go check out English Bay, the gateway into the North Pacific Ocean. It was not far down the street, and perhaps I'd gather some intel on a local oyster joint. First things first, though.

"I'll take a Double Vera with fries, please."

After I was finished, I felt like an anaconda just finishing off its prey, belly about to burst due to ingesting a third of its body weight. I needed to either walk it off or sleep for three days. I didn't have time for a three-day slumber, so I headed out the door. I hung a right and headed for English Bay, which wasn't far down the quaint, shop-lined street.

Flying in earlier in the day, clear skies had allowed for a view of the bay. It was no match in size to the Pacific Ocean that it fed? Not that it mattered. It was large enough to handle every manner of craft, from sailboat to tanker; it was substantial. All this was so new to me. I'd never even seen a tanker. These damn things were as big as my hometown. Awe-inspiring. A long stone wall, a couple of feet in height, seemed like a great place to sit and ponder. Looking over the bay, I imagined the destination of the sailboat I saw there, its mast rising twenty, maybe thirty feet into the air. Was it a day trip or a further multiday exploration they set their sails for? The tanker brought a larger vision. Something so massive had to be traveling some distance. I imagined stowing away, traveling the high seas and exploring distant lands. Discovered too late to be sent back, I'd be allowed to stay on board and earn my keep. They'd dump me at some faraway port to fend for myself. How I'd return home was of little concern in my imagined drama. My inner hobo had been awakened, and I felt a heightened sense of wonder.

I have yet to experience the freshness of a Hawaiian pineapple or a mango picked and eaten in the Philippines. I'd been fortunate to taste the cherries of Washington State, fresh from the tree. They were so sweet, so amazingly alive, that I gorged for days, stopping just before I ate my way to a hatred of them. I can't be sure what the cherries were that I had bought before, back home in Iowa. They said "cherries," but that must have been a misprint. I'll assume all other fresh-from-the-tree experiences are similar. On my way to a hotel bar recommended to me by a friend who shared my love of oysters, I planned to put the freshness theory to the test once again.

"Right out there, man. These bad boys were pulled out of the water yesterday," the bartender let me know, laying six oysters on the half shell in front of me with horseradish and a lemon wedge on the side. A small amount of what he called "mignonette sauce" accompanied the arrangement. These oysters were practically the size of my head. "Doctor 'em up however you like, or not at all. It's your world, buddy."

The bartender and I were getting along swimmingly. He was stoked to have a wide-eyed Midwesterner in front of him. The pride he had in these half-shelled beauties was evident. In taste, they equaled or even exceeded what their impressive appearance promised. Another half dozen were ordered before the second one had even found its way atop a cracker.

Looking out over the bay, I saw the sun closing the distance to the horizon, and I was reminded that there was one more task I needed to address: I had no place to sleep. The bartender's knowledge of oysters and other local fare unfortunately did not extend to hostels. Vagabonds were not often the type to order oysters in fancy hotel bars, apparently. A couple hundred bucks, and I could call it a night right there in the hotel. But a couple hundred bucks was about all I had to my name. With eight days remaining, I thanked the bartender for the experience and set out on the day's final mission: cheap sleep.

I walked and walked. Finding a hostel was proving to be a challenge. This being my first hostel treasure hunt, I did not know what to expect. "Excuse me, would you know of any hostels in the area?" Strike one. Next passerby, same. Strike two. Again. Strike three. *Hmm.* The thought occurred to me that perhaps I should just go "hobo." A nearby park with a picnic table would do the trick. I feared, though, that this nearly immaculate city might frown on such things, and the thought of being rousted from my sleep by the Royal Canadian Mounted Police didn't sit well with me. Incurring any sort of squatter's fine would defeat the cheap sleep mission.

A close second concern was making it as easy as possible to be found in the morning. I'd hoofed it a couple of miles and did not want to go much further, for fear my cabbie from earlier in the day might struggle to find me this far from our original drop point. I decided to make a couple left turns at the next opportunity and continued the search, headed back toward where I had come. The goal was to be able to get myself back to the exact place of my drop off first thing in the morning and keep things easy for my cab-driving friend.

With the sun about to retire for the day, I was growing a bit nervous. The big city at night was daunting. It would be good to find a place to lay my head sooner rather than later. A couple blocks off the main drag, the city lost some of its luster, which was good—and bad. Good in that if I needed to go the hotel route it would be less money. Bad in that as night approached there was a sense, perhaps imagined, that the streets were becoming a bit more wild, and a traveler with all his possessions on his back would make an obvious target for anyone with larceny in his heart.

The not-entirely-working light hanging off the not-entirely-maintained brick building read "Ho el." *This might be the place*, I thought. If the establishment couldn't afford or didn't care enough to replace the burnt-out T in their sign, maybe they'd have a room that would fit my budget.

"Fifty-three dollars with tax" the well-pierced, black-haired receptionist informed me.

"Your over fifty, right?"

A bit slow on the uptake, but not too slow, I responded, "Of course. I work out…a lot. I'm very young for my age."

"Then it's forty-five dollars with your AARP." I got the feeling she really enjoyed sticking it to "the man" and the establishment she worked for.

Cheap sleep. Not hostel cheap, but still, mission accomplished. Tomorrow, the Yukon.

Chapter 23

"I'll be at the exact spot you dropped me yesterday. How's that sound?"

I'd wondered if my cabbie from the day prior would actually answer the call, seeing how it was just a bit past 6:00 a.m. The fear of being carried away by roaches combined with the excitement of the day that waited for me had made the hotel wake-up call unnecessary. But it was as if he had been waiting all morning, wondering the same. Would the vagabond kayaker make good on his side of the deal? He had picked up.

"You bet. See you there at seven? Great day for an adventure!" he replied.

Dreams, once realized, are never as they were envisioned. It is impossible to nail every detail when looking into a crystal ball. But my cabbie materialized and whisked me back to the airport to the Air North gate.

The gate was near the end of the airport. Air North does not share the same list of amenities you get when flying American, United, or Southwest. I walked down a flight of metal stairs; my footsteps echoed off the stark white cement walls, notifying all below of my impending arrival. It was perfect. Not at all what I had imagined, but perfect nonetheless. There were no TVs sharing news of the day. The gate attendant wore a heavy three-quarter-length wool coat. Temperatures were easily twenty degrees cooler than the main floor of the airport. Outside, there was no enclosed Jetway to shield passengers from the elements. Just beyond the attendant, a drafty glass door swung open as some of the service personnel came in and out. Summer was near, but Vancouver in early June could still put a chill into you.

"Air North, Flight 386 to Whitehorse is now ready to board."

There were no groups one, two, and three. I'd guess there were only twenty folks waiting at most. Looking them over, I wondered if any shared my reasons for heading to this faraway place. None jumped out as fellow adventurers, but you never know. Appearances can be most deceiving. Cliché or not, judging a book by its cover often leads to leaving an amazing book unread.

The bundled-up attendant, taking my ticket, offered up the usual, "Enjoy your trip to the Yukon, Mr. Cannon."

God, I loved the sound of that! Pushing the handle, the door swung open, and a crisp, northern breeze smacked me in the face. Not the sort of smack that shocks you into pain and anger, but rather the cheerful, refreshing kind of smack that only Mother Nature can provide. Invigorating, but wonderful. Stopping for just a moment, letting the couple behind me pass, I inhaled deeply, eyes closed, imagining its journey. This breeze was my breeze. It had originated some time ago. How long ago, I was unsure. It had left the mountains of the great north, gathering speed as it passed over the Yukon River and countless other geographical landmarks, destined for the adventurer from Iowa who had dared to dream of this far-off land, and now it had found me. For the first time, I felt the great Yukon's spirit.

Chapter 24

Sputtering slightly at first, the two propeller engines roared to life. The window seat, which I had made sure to request so many months ago—seemingly a different life ago—offered a perfect vantage point: seat 16D. I was two rows behind the wings and the now-roaring props, and my seat shook a bit. There were maybe twenty rows in total. Not a big plane by today's modern standards, it was still sizable for the Yukon. Letting my mind wander, I imagined it would have inspired awe in those who had settled and gold-rushed the territories so many years before. In a land where the wild things out-numbered the civilized, it was fitting to travel this last leg by prop plane.

I was going to the world's longest kayak race to test myself, physically and mentally, but I'd also embarked on this adventure to find simplicity. The Yukon and its race would offer, I hoped, an opportunity to leave *civil*-ization and all its mind trappings be-hind. There is so much daily clutter—TV, email, internet, politics, soap operas, work, deadlines. If not aware, we can easily become lost in all of that, become swallowed up by it. *Where on that list is time that is set aside only for you?* Don't pass this question without pause—and an honest answer.

Past adventures had allowed me a glimpse of myself. The time I'd be spending in the Yukon camping, exploring, immersing myself in all things Whitehorse, and, eventually, taking on the great river would allow me to once again spend time with just me.

Unencumbered by all of the mind-sucks everyday life can offer, the call of this simple land was intoxicating.

The props bit into the wind, grasping for purchase as the flaps, now set at the correct angle, brought the nose off the ground. Vancouver's grip—indeed, society's grip—strained to hold me. The battle being waged between our two-prop plane and gravity was a metaphor for my own battle. Safety, status quo, and all of civilization's comforts strove to keep me in the fold, but my spirit refused. Uncertainty, adventure, and the unknown, accompanied by both excitement and fear, refused to be held down.

A great spirit lives in us all. Ignore it for too long, and its voice will become too faint to hear. Rejoice though, for it never dies. You need only to dare, to dream, and it awakens in an instant from its slumber. Find your adventure. Fire up your props. Let your nose, and in turn your glance, rise toward the clouds. Life is not meant to be lived safely. It is meant to be *lived*! Fly, fly, *fly*! To your Yukon, FLY!

Chapter 25

HAVE YOU EVER EXPERIENCED SOMETHING SO FREAKING DELICIOUS, wonderful, and exhilarating that it defies your best attempts at description? How frustrating it is to lack the appropriate language skills to describe a sunset over the Rockies. Each moment, the sun changes the canvas. The clouds above, slightly scattered, changing chameleon-like—orangish, reddish, purplish hues in constant flux, the views stealing each of your breaths as you watch the scene unfold.

How does one describe love? Certainly, there are those who have made a run at it, but even those poets with hearts wide open, sitting and penning at their very best will go mad if their goal is any real semblance of the feeling itself. What a conundrum. Full of awe and excitement, friends' ears at the ready, we attempt to share. The energy thrums; our audience can sense it, their sense of adventure hungry for the upcoming meal.

How could you really explain with any substance the homemade cinnamon rolls that Betsy makes? Betsy is eighty-two years old. The recipe is, I can only imagine, much older than she. The slight tint of red within the swirls of the decadent homemade frosting suggests cherry may be involved. My best go at this would be to tell you that your granny's cherry pie and your auntie's cinnamon roll got together one late night, and what Betsy has created at the Milk Pail in Rice Lake, Wisconsin, is their secret love child. A taste-bud-blowing combination of all things yummy.

English Bay and the city of Vancouver had long left my view. I can only wish for you, and it is my ultimate wish for you, that what I felt and what I saw out the airplane window that day is something that you will experience many, many times over. The Indian poet and mystic Sadhguru Jaggi Vasudev once said:

> People come to me thirsty, thirsty for how to find peace, how to find joy, fulfillment, excitement in everyday life. I do not see it my purpose to quench that thirst, but rather to increase it, to share all that I can about what can be so they become so parched they search these things for themselves. If they seek, they will find.

Adventurers before me—some I've known personally, others I've known through book or film; some real, some fictional—had stirred the pot for me and awakened the beast, as it were. Their stories left me dry mouthed. To quench that thirst meant I'd have to strike out on my own. Planning, talking, reading, and watching were temporary fixes. The real well, endless in its supply, was experience. Why take just a sip when you can immerse yourself entirely in the water?

Perfect. Even this word, supposedly the be-all and end-all in describing the ultimate, falls short. It was as if the snow-white peaks below were a perfect match for the wispy, pristine clouds that danced above them and just slightly below me. Or were the peaks a perfect reflection of the clouds just beyond their reach? No matter. The grandeur of the view was beyond the scope of comprehension. The land below was so wild, untouched. The chances seemed high that as far as my glance would allow, no human had ever trodden. *Ever.* More folks had stepped foot on the moon than this place we flew over. This was an original. It was the Sistine Chapel, the *Mona Lisa.* It was Beethoven's Fifth and so much more. It was creation. It was Mother Nature's genius stroke. Tomorrow, she may wave her paintbrush, choosing one more stroke on her canvas, and just like that, a new masterpiece would be revealed. I imagined Wolf, the alpha predator presiding over these lands, taking part in a great dance that included Moose, Badger, and all things wild. This place, where I could not fathom even attempting mere survival, was what they called home. It struck me then that this place held an element of timelessness. As long as I walk this earth and for as long as those who come after me walk this earth, this land over which we were flying would continue to flourish, beyond human reach. The dense forests, taking the hands of streams imperceptible from this altitude, moving in counterpoint with the hills and mountains, would together continue their dance until the end of time. Even time itself seemed to lose meaning during this contemplation.

Am I making you thirsty? Can you *feel* the view as the props carry us over the Yukon Territory? To see it, which I have tried to portray for you here as best I could, is one thing; that will quench your thirst for a bit. To truly feel it, to drink it in fully, you must experience it physically. You must immerse yourself in it.

The tenor of the props changed slightly; a decrease in speed followed.

"Good day, everyone. We are beginning our descent into Whitehorse. The attendant will be by to collect any items you wish to discard. Looking down, I realized I hadn't taken even one sip from my glass of water. The symbolism was not lost on me. For the time being, it appeared my thirst had been quenched.

Chapter 26

I HAVE BECOME A COLLECTOR OF BREATHS. MOST OF MY LIFE, this was not so. The first breath that comes to mind? After six and a half days in jail—it would have been seven, but I had credit for time served—my life abruptly changed course. The Johnson County Hilton, also known as the Iowa City jail, had housed me for nearly a week after my second drunk driving offense. Reflecting, I may have been the only "guest" not raging against my circumstances.

The character known as Red in *The Shawshank Redemption* shook his head and responded that he was the "only guilty man in Shawshank" in response to Andy Dufresne's coyly asked question, "What about you? What are you in for...innocent?" There was a peace about Red, and while there was no difference in appearance from the other inmates, there was a difference in vibe. So it was with me. There were at least one million other places I'd have rather been, but none where I more needed to be. It was a necessary step—the first of many, perhaps a lifetime's worth of steps—to find myself. I may have been the only "guilty" man in that jail. I was there only because of me. Not because my dad hadn't loved me enough, not because the kids at school had picked on me, not because I hadn't grown up with this or that. I was there because I had made a mess of my life. I've since learned everyone has a story. Some soar regardless; some don't. What do they all have in common? They did so because they chose to. I was damn lucky to be alive. Newly sober and with a clearer head, I was grateful beyond words to have another go at this thing called life.

The sky was clear outside the jail but for a few wispy clouds. From the southeast blew a slight breeze. Looking to the sky, I gave it my attention for the first time since I was a youth full of wonder at the base of the split spruce in my front yard. The breeze took hold of me gently, pulling me in as if to say, "We've got you now; it's all gonna be OK." I felt its warm embrace, turning to face it. Emptying my lungs and inhaling deeply, I collected my first breath. To this day I can return to that exact place as vividly as I describe it now, knowing still that I am safe in the arms of the universe.

I have added many breaths to my collection since. The breath from the top of Mount Evans, the highest paved road in North America at just over 14,000 feet, after riding my bike to its summit. The breath while in my mother's welcoming arms, having just run 1,037 miles around the Great Lake Michigan. A similar, yet unique breath after tackling my first run across my beautiful home state of Iowa. The deep breath necessary after dancing naked and free around the fire, camping out of view of all but the coyote or the buffalo deep in the recesses of the Badlands. The frosty breath that fogged my goggles on the Tuscobia 150 Winter Ultra, forcing me to remove them as I looked overhead, temperature well below zero, my location known to no one, the stars so very bright, and trees occasionally popping as the cold cut into them.

* * *

Where are you right now? Are you sitting in a favorite coffee shop that soothes your need for caffeine and provides you with a space to meet friends, a place where the barista know you always order a "medium latte, whole milk, one shot"? Are you perhaps sitting in admiration of the coffee in front of you as it cools just enough to take your first sip? Perhaps you are... sitting in a chair that isn't particularly pretty but is too comfy to discard, placed next to the west-facing window in the den so you can capture the setting sun as you prepare to call it a day. Or maybe you're just catching a few minutes of reading as the gas tank fills because this is the greatest book you have ever read; even an hour away from it leaves your soul aching just a bit. I especially like that last one.

Whatever the case, I invite you, I challenge you, I double dog dare you, to collect a breath right now. Take a few deep preparatory breaths. Center. Find yourself. I'm talking about the real you, the adventurous you, the dreamer and believer-in-all-things-possible you. What is that one thing that has laid in wait for much too long? What is the one thing that's always there, but just behind making the kids lunch, or going to the grocery store, or working, or retiring? What is that one "as soon as I finish this task or that task" thing, that inevitably gets delayed when another task appears, keeping your one thing always the next thing? Let this next breath be the one when you put your one thing in first place. Commit to starting now. What is the first step? No matter how insignificant it may seem, do it. You are on your way. Now, you are ready for step two, then three...You have done it! You have placed you first, perhaps for the first time in some time. Remember that breath, for it was the one that started it all. One you will never forget.

Chapter 27

"An adventure is an exciting or unusual experience. It may also be a bold, usually risky undertaking, with an uncertain outcome," says the Wikipedia entry for the word. A bold, usually risky undertaking, with outcome uncertain. What would the world look like, what would your world look like, if this word *adventure* were replaced with *life*? What if this definition was offered up by Wikipedia when one typed *life* into the Google search window?

I wondered what Wikipedia might say about life as I sat here typing these words in the Coffee Loft. "The definition of life is controversial. The current definition is that organisms maintain homeostasis, are composed of cells, undergo metabolism, can grow, adapt to their environment, respond to stimuli, and reproduce." I think that lacks a bit of excitement and pizzazz. Wouldn't you agree?

I am not debating the Wikipedia definition. To be honest, I was unable to read the entirety of the entry on *life*. It bored me. Adventure, however? I read that definition in its entirety. It went on:

> Adventures may be activities with some potential for physical danger such as traveling, exploring, skydiving, mountain climbing, scuba diving, river rafting, or participating in extreme sports. The term also broadly refers to any enterprise that is potentially fraught with physical, financial, or psychological risk, such as a business venture, or other major life undertakings.

I found myself smiling. Wikipedia, devoid of emotion in all definitions, had sounded damn near poetic ... I can only imagine, to its own frustration.

An unusually crisp, cool breeze followed the lowering of the plane door onto the tarmac. Exhilarating! I was breathing the air of the Yukon for the first time. Like so many before me seeking adventure, I had finally found my way to this until-now mythical place. Anticipation, excitement, fear, and uncertainty—all at heightened levels—made the simple act of releasing the seat belt latch a bit of a challenge. I felt like a young child tearing into that first Christmas present in the morning. It should have been easy to just pull off the tape from one end of the box, then the other, releasing the wrapping paper. Instead, unbridled joy and enthusiasm found me tearing at the paper, fumbling with the box, turning the very simple act of unwrapping a present into something much more difficult. So it was with the seat belt. I had looked over this countryside from my window seat for too long, the beautiful valleys and peaks like wrapping paper below, taunting me.

Like my mother reminding me over the years, "It's not time yet, Steven. You have to wait till everyone's ready," the plane door had stood between me and the Yukon. Now it lay open, its stairs descending to the asphalt runway. It was time to rip into my present. I had travelled on much larger planes, though not often. If I were to guess, those planes had held 100 to 200 people. Our flight contained fewer than twenty, yet it seemed to take an eternity for them to get the hell out of my way and off that plane.

"Welcome to Whitehorse...Welcome to Whitehorse...Welcome to Whitehorse ... "

"Thank you...Thank you...Thank you."

Each exchange before me seemed as generic as any daily greeting one may receive each day at work, said more out of duty and responded to in kind.

A favorite saying of mine is, "Wherever two smiles meet, God is awoken." The stewardess prepared to hit me with her dutiful "Welcome to Whitehorse" when I hit her right between the eyes with the smile of a five-year-old at the Christmas tree. Helpless to fight instinct, her face came to life. After just a slight pause, she delivered her "Welcome to Whitehorse" with emotion. I accepted it with an enthusiastic "Thank you!" I'd like to think that she truly felt my gratitude for her part in delivering me safely to this place. Standing on the top step, the entirety of the Yukon lay before me. It struck me that for the next nine days, every step, every paddle stroke would be into the unknown.

"An adventure is an exciting or unusual experience. It may also be a bold, usually risky undertaking, with an uncertain outcome."

Stepping into the Whitehorse airport, I headed for the baggage carousel to fetch up my backpack. It wasn't evident to me then as it is now. I was redefining my life. I had decided to trade the known, the paths followed by so many before me, safe and certain, for the unknown, and it had led me to this place. What I could not have forecasted was that doing so might end me.

Chapter 28

"Kanoe People, First and Strickland," I replied to the cabbie's inquiry of "Where to, traveler?"

His phrasing had a nice ring to it. *This dude will be getting a nice tip*, I thought. Sliding my right arm out of the shoulder strap, the backpack came free, allowing me to swing it off the left shoulder and give it a toss into the backseat before I followed in after it.

Scott McDougall and his wife Joanne were the owners of Kanoe People and had been since 1974. Their shop, with the Yukon River running wild just behind it, had a real Yukon look to it online. There were a couple of other kayak rental locations offered up on the race site, and I'm sure they all do a great job. I wouldn't know though. Scott had won me off right out of the gate. A few email exchanges, followed by a call or two, and I felt right at home with him. Patient and eager to assist a wide-eyed, wannabe adventurer from Iowa, there was no need to interview other providers. I mean, come on, someone guiding people on the Yukon River for over thirty some years, operating out of an A-frame cabin, cast against the backdrop of the great river? How can that be beat?

It was a relatively short drive from Erik Nielsen Whitehorse International Airport. I thanked the driver and tossed him three extra dollars, which was the equivalent of a twenty using the dirt-poor adventurer/wealthy traveler exchange rate. If all went according to plan—though I'd already begun to realize that adventures never do, and I've learned to love that about them—I would return home with a couple hundred bucks left to my name. That made the tip something like 1.5 percent of my net worth. Ideally, this would be the last real modern comfort I'd enjoy. Freeze-dried meals and prepacked candy bars would serve as sustenance while here, the tent strapped to the bottom of the pack would be home, and the two feet below me the mode of transportation. Operation "Yukon Submersion" was on. With the shutting of the cab door behind me, I slung the pack over my left shoulder and, with a hula-hoop-like swing of the hips, I was able to navigate my right arm through the strap. A little hop brought both straps into position over my shoulders.

Time to meet Scott and the gang and get this party started, I thought. It was pretty surreal standing there, Kanoe People right in front of me, and beyond that the mighty Yukon River. The store excited me; the river evoked a different mix of emotions entirely.

My home state of Iowa claims a portion of the Mississippi River. The "Ol' Man" is no joke. Running nearly the entirety of the United States north to south, it more than holds its own in the discussion of great rivers. Perhaps it was the surroundings, the immense, rugged Yukon Territory, that made the difference. Hard men had come here in search of adventure, some for fortune. Hard men, much harder than me, if I were to be honest with myself, had died here in those pursuits. Perhaps it was the speed at which she flowed or her temperature—never, ever, warm. This place, these waters, offered adventure in spades, but looking it in the face brought the reality of it all to me, and made me pause to think, *What the hell have I gotten myself into?*

Canoes, kayaks, transportation vans—the place had it all. Once inside, the building felt more like a log cabin than a retail or boat rental shop. Scott, as luck would have it, was the first person to greet me. We exchanged our hellos.

He beat me to the punch. "Steve Cannon." Before I could add my origin, he jumped right in, "Yeah, from Iowa, eh? Glad you made it, man. How was the trip? You excited?"

And just like that, a thousand miles from Des Moines, it felt as if I'd been welcomed into the tribe. We chatted about this thing and that. The weather dominated much of the early conversation. It had been an unusually wet and cold spring. The race takes place during the time of the "midnight sun," a season when darkness never totally falls. For a few hours each day, the sun, when not obstructed by the occasional rain clouds, takes a nap, leaving a sort of dusk in its place. I was interested to see the effect, if any, that days with no darkness might have on my internal clock.

Clients came and went. I was in no hurry, and Scott was totally cool with my just hanging out and soaking up the place. There was nothing pending, other than a short hike through town to the campground I'd staked out as my temporary home months prior from the comfort of my apartment in Des Moines.

Most folks racing would be arriving over the next few days, although a couple stopped in while I hung out, both having done the race in prior years. Scott introduced me as "Steve from Iowa, here for his first kayak race." He wasn't really saying, *Look at this greenhorn; what does he think he's doing?* but rather, *Ain't it great? That's the spirit!* I, however, hearing the introduction, got a chill and wondered for the second time in as many hours, *Am I in over my head here?* It is said that the biggest idiot is the idiot who doesn't know he's an idiot. Again, I squelched that inner dialogue. I had no lack of respect for this place; quite the opposite. Reminding myself that real adventure required an uncertainty of outcome, I bid Scott and his crew thanks for their time. We set a date to try out kayaks tomorrow.

I'd decided (or rather, my pocketbook had decided) not to ship my kayak from home, which meant I'd be using a new boat on race day. "Never try something new on race day" is a cardinal rule. But I'd figured that with Scott's guidance, I'd get into a similar craft. That decision had nagged me from the moment it had been made so many months prior. It nagged more now. Leaving Kanoe People and a few worries behind, I headed into Whitehorse, on my way to the campground to see what I could see. The race was a large part of why I was here, but it was not the only part. Tomorrow I would once again return to Kanoe People and be "Steve from Iowa, doing his first kayak race." The longest kayak and canoe race in the world. *Gulp.* The rest of today, however, I would be "Steve from Iowa, Whitehorse and Yukon Territory explorer."

Chapter 29

IT HAD TAKEN LESS THAN TWO HOURS. IN LESS THAN TWO HOURS, the folks at Kanoe People, local clients, a few fellow racers, and an adventurer from Germany had me feeling right at home. I would come to realize a truth about this place during my stay. Whitehorse, to the outsider, and at times I'm sure even to those that call it home, is a tough place to live. As I type these words, sitting in the Badger Brew Coffee Loft in Rice Lake, Wisconsin, it's a balmy thirty-seven degrees in Whitehorse. It's January sixteenth. I'd bet money there's a local in Whitehorse going about his business there in a pair of Carhartt shorts, weathered flannel, and work boots that have seen many a hard winter over a pair of thick wool socks. That's because typically temps are consistently below zero this time of year. A week before I write this, lows in Whitehorse were in the minus-thirty-degree range. Most of us shudder to think of those temperatures. Those that call Whitehorse home endure far colder for far longer.

Looking out for one another was something that had been bred into their culture. The people in Whitehorse embodied the "it takes a village" approach to life. Already I could sense a pride in those I'd met, a genuine pleasure at visitors to the town, as well as a willingness to share the fabric of Whitehorse in totality. I was suspicious of this at first but can confirm it now. Gold, silver…those were not the treasures to be found in the Yukon. It was the people. I sensed immediately that if you were willing to come to this place, be it to work, play, adventure, or take the test the Quest offered, that was enough. You were welcomed with open arms.

I was hungry and still had a couple of miles to tote myself and my pack to camp. Thinking that this would be a most appropriate time to treat myself, I decided my first meal in Whitehorse would not be a freeze-dried one, cooked inside a "magic bag" that required only boiling water from my stove to ready the goods inside. Nope, that simply would not do on this monumental occasion. I did not come to the decision lightly, however. The thought of boiling water, the Yukon drizzle shielded by my tent's vestibule, and preparing my first meal seated cross-legged just inside my tent also seemed wholly appropriate. My growling belly cast the deciding vote. Sometimes, he who yells loudest does win. This was one of those times. Walking the few blocks southwest from Kanoe People toward downtown, there was no denying that calories would be nice before hiking south along Robert Service Way to the campground bearing the same name, which would be my home for the trip.

There were so many cool things to see, each requiring a bit of pause. Following Front Street, keeping the great river to my left, I came upon the Miles Canyon Historic Railway Society. The society's stated purpose is "to restore and preserve mining and railway history of the Yukon." Hop on the trolley tour offered, and you could check out Spook Creek Station, Shipyards Park, the White Pass & Yukon Route depot, and the SS Klondike National Historic Site.

Come on! I thought. *Are you kidding me? How cool is this place?!*

Every stop described, and these were just a few, only stoked my curiosity and spirit of adventure further. I wanted to see and experience it all.

Walking the streets of Whitehorse felt like riding an interactive time machine. If you look and also do not look, the history of the place can be seen and, indeed, felt. So-called modern necessities, banks and historic buildings redone, provide a superficial mask to the reality and history of Whitehorse and the Yukon Territory as a whole. Amazing murals cover entire building sides throughout the downtown. Each tells a story, be it the gold rush, the sternwheeler, the musher, or the Royal Canadian Mounted Police. My favorite was an amazingly vibrant piece on the side of an old elementary school building. The mural depicted the land of the Yukon and its most famous inhabitants: grand, majestic, rugged peaks; the head of a wolf deftly hidden; and the grizzly bear tending to her cub as the bald eagle soared effortlessly above. Were it not for the nagging of my stomach, there is no telling how long I'd have stood in awe, not just of the mural, but that I was, for now, a part of it all.

Chapter 30

G&P STEAKHOUSE & PIZZA CAUGHT MY EYE SOON AFTER MAKING a right turn onto Main Street. "Steakhouse & Pizza" does not do their menu justice. Thinking back to the famous scene from the film *Jerry Maguire*, even with all sorts of extraordinary fare jumping off the pages, I thought, *They had me at "pizza."* Combined with their "Come in as guests, leave as friends" theme, which in just a few hours I'd realized was the theme of the whole damn town, the menu made me certain I'd found the right place to silence the growl in my stomach.

Like a cat stalking his next nap, I did my best not to let a single detail get by me. As soon as the front door opened, welcoming me in, I took in the lighting, the smell of the place, and the folks at the tables.

Hmm...the two dudes a few tables to the left, closer to the windows. They ain't locals, I thought.

The fit body and hard jawline could have belonged to any Yukon man. It's doubtful this place is home to many slackers. But it was the clothing, more "race-y" than what one would expect of a local, that caught my glance first off. Listening a little confirmed my suspicions. I'm no expert in linguistics, but the accent was British, I thought, and with three or four sentences in a row, none ending with "eh," I was betting money I'd found a couple of Questers. I wasn't the only one taking stock. Both men had glanced over upon my walking in, sort of like we were in a spaghetti Western, maybe sizing me up as well. I wouldn't go so far as to say the music in the place stopped as I entered, a la Clint Eastwood, but there was a meeting of the eyes, followed by a respectful nod of the head. The backpack, still slung over both my shoulders, and my full beard, grown for the first time in my life to get me as much into a rugged state of mind, along with the jacket I wore, sporting a few race patches, probably set off their racer radar as well.

They were just partly correct, if those indeed were their assumptions. The only real mistake they would have made was pegging me for a racer. Sure, I was here *for* the race, but not to *win* the race. The Quest was a huge mouthful for me to bite off. Finishing was my *only* goal. Survival, I'd soon find out, should also have been high on the list.

While not being the Old Wild West, Whitehorse was still mostly wild and west, and the fact that the two blokes were not like the rest of the clientele—in canvas work pants, multi-tools firmly attached to belt straps, fully engrossed in their discussions, and not looking up upon my entrance into the place—invited a meeting that just might prove rewarding.

What I was about to find out was these guys *were* here to race—and to race for the win. *Screw it*, I thought. *Nothing ventured, nothing gained.* Taking a few steps their way, both seemed welcoming in their facial expressions, the shorter of the two men a bit more so than his buddy.

"Here for the River Quest?"

"Yep. You too?" I replied.

"Yep. Pull up a seat if ya like."

I did. Immediately I felt a sense of kinship from the two men. We started chatting.

"Where're you from?"

"Des Moines, Iowa. You?"

"Jersey, Channel Islands."

I thought to myself, *Huh? Best to keep my mouth shut in place of opening and revealing my ignorance.* But hey, what did I have to protect? Just my damn ego. So I let it rip.

"Huh? That sounds like a really cool place. Where the hell is it?"

This got a good laugh and a super-interesting start to what would be a couple hours of conversation. Turns out, Jersey is the largest of the islands located in the channel between England and France. Rowing is a big deal in Jersey, and these two were a big part of its long, proud history.

Rob was the more talkative of the two; Carl seemed pleasant but also content to let Rob lead. Carl intimidated me a bit. I'm six feet, three inches, around 195 pounds, and pretty damn fit. I felt small next to the man. He had a presence to him, one I was unsure of at first. He proved to be not only a man of superior strength and high intelligence—he was a doctor back home—but also a genuine teddy bear and very caring. Rob worked for the coast guard and was one charismatic fellow. He was the type of person who consumed life in the largest of quantities possible. He looked to me like the kind of dude who would emerge from the bottom of a rugby scrum with the tenacity of a badger, ball firmly in his grasp; I guessed the smile and good looks belied a real toughness.

Their stories confirmed all. Years prior, in 1997, the two had completed what was then known as simply The Atlantic Rowing Race, now known as The Talisker Whisky Atlantic Challenge. That year, the race went from Tenerife to Barbados, more than three thousand nautical miles. Before their completion of the race, fewer than thirty successful ocean rows had been completed. Ever. Holy shit. I was not sure if the words actually came out of my mouth. I was in the presence of freaking paddling Jedis. I suddenly felt amazingly, embarrassingly, out of place. What had I done? What could I possibly have been thinking? Rob and Carl were giants in this game. I'm no history buff, but they had accomplished a feat on par with walking on the damn moon as far as successful attempts were concerned. To throw gasoline on top of my panic fire, this race, in their own words, "scared the shit out of them." They wouldn't stop talking about how they hoped to just finish. They had come here as a team, with years of paddling in their bodies and hundreds, if not thousands, of experience hours, and they just hoped to finish? I was here to take on the river solo.

Jesus freaking Christ! That was not said aloud, but I'm sure the full-on freakout was showing on my face. I'd paddled the Iowa River, Lake Red Rock, and some twenty-four- and thirty-six-hour adventure races. Back home, I was the guy pushing limits. Or so I had thought.

Welcome to the big leagues, I thought. Suddenly I was a character in *Bull Durham,* having hit forty-eight home runs in high school, chest puffed out, swinging and missing at the first three heaters I saw in spring training. Completely overmatched. Not back in Iowa anymore.

Welcome to the big leagues, indeed.

"Holy shit" was the name of the broken record playing in my mind. But even though I kept kicking the old Victrola over and over again, I could not get it to stop playing. I didn't hold all of my angst inside, and the boys were quick to try and quell my fears, perhaps sensing my panic. Due to their extensive experience, they were undoubtedly thinking, *Damn, this kid's got balls...balls that might get him in big trouble.*

I was all too happy to change the topic. Carl and Rob were great storytellers, proud of the things they had done together and where they came from. We shared many more stories. Well, they shared mostly, as I was all too keen to learn about Jersey, these two bigger-than-life paddlers, their adventures, and their conquests, which were many. For a time, my fears subsided. We agreed to a Kanoe People meetup the following day for our first go at the mighty Yukon River.

Chapter 31

IT WAS BELOW ZERO, AND THERE WERE MAYBE EIGHT INCHES OF snow on the Tuscobia trail. I had time for a pre-ride before the race kicked off 6:00 a.m. the next morning.

A few months prior on a whim and with a couple of inches of fresh snow, I had taken a Salsa Mukluk Fat Bike for a ride down one of our local bike trails. I'd done so to prove a point: that these bikes with their four- and five-inch-wide tires were nothing more than another passing fad. A few friends had them, and their adventures bushwhacking on two wheels or touring the sandy lakefront did seem fun. But if I were to be completely honest, secretly I mocked them. Taking to the trail, the fresh layer of snow not yet touched, I made the first tracks. That was always cool, be it on skis, snowshoes, or even, I admitted, a fat bike. The trail, mostly straight, meandered here and there, tree-lined, between crop fields. It was eight miles round-trip. That's all it took. I was eating my words en masse. If indeed fat bikes were a passing fad, then I'd be a sucker like the rest, but a happy sucker, riding over and through anything and everything. The boys at Rasmussen Bike Shop had seen this all before and got a good laugh upon my return.

Seeing the joy the oversized two-wheeler had brought me, they met my grin with a "Ready to buy it? The joke is that if you ride one, you'll buy one. We knew you'd be hooked for sure, dude." They were right. I went from mocker to owner in eight miles.

Less than a month later, I signed up for The Tuscobia Winter Ultra, which went from Park Falls, Wisconsin, to Rice Lake, Wisconsin, and back. With no winter ultra experience under my belt, I had to get a friend to vouch for me and assure the race directors that I wouldn't die. You can't just sign up for this race. Temperatures can drop well below zero. Required gear includes things like stoves, fuel, three thousand calories of food, and at least a minus-twenty-degree sleeping bag. It's made mighty clear that if you find yourself in trouble, you'd better be able to "bivvy" (set up a very quick shelter) and wait for help to arrive.

Five pedal strokes. That's how far my prerace dress rehearsal lasted on the trail before I dumped the bike on its side, falling in a heap right next to it. Looking around, I made sure no one saw that. No one did. I steadied the bike again. *Must have been a patch of ice underneath the snow,* I thought. Sliding all over the place, unable to control it, I made it another ten feet or so before bam, I was down again.

Snow is not too common in Iowa anymore. My inaugural ride had been my first and last in snow until then.

This is not good, I was thinking. *One hundred and fifty miles, and I can't go ten feet without dumping.*

Math was my best subject, but it escaped me to figure out how many falls there were in one hundred and fifty miles, taken ten feet at a time. All of this would be taking place over what was forecasted to be between minus five and minus ten degrees. How that race turned out is a subject for another time. For now, the point is this: leaving the restaurant that day, after hearing Rob and Carl's accomplishments, stories, and angst over the impending event, backpack securely again over both shoulders, I thought, much like that day in Wisconsin, brushing the snow off all parts of my body, *Shit, what have I gotten myself into?*

The happy-go-lucky adventurer who had entered the doors just an hour earlier was now headed for the campground feeling much less happy and lucky. By the time I'd walked the few blocks back toward the river and followed the path south toward the campground, my head started to clear. Never give a person too much credit, or too little. The same could be said for adventures or personal challenges. Too many dreams are shot dead before they start: killed one bullet a time, fired from the guns of well-meaning family and friends.

"What about this? What about that? You can't do that! What about your kids, your wife, your job?"

Bang. Bang. Bang. Bang-bang-bang.

And just like that, a dream dies before it even starts, stalled into submission by the doubts and concerns of others. Advice and concerns are not without value, but in the end, it's your dream, and your belief wins the day. If you believe in your gut, do not be swayed by outside influences. History is full of incredible accomplishments that were once deemed by others to be impossible.

The very river that brought a cold, northerly sweat to me moments before while sitting in the restaurant with Carl and Rob now soothed me as I walked along her banks.

* * *

"Sometimes, you just die," the man had said.

The man's Humvee had been stuck on a remote mountainside when my friend Bjorn came across him quite by accident. Bjorn was on the road by virtue of some less-than-well-thought-out decisions. This man with the Humvee, named Rob, was massive, or so the story went. He and his German shepherd dog had spent the previous fifteen years or so searching remote mountain passes in the western United States, hired by some branch of the U.S. government to report where, if we were some day attacked, the aggressors might come from. By all accounts, the meeting was a rare one. One got the feeling that "Rob" (Bjorn doubted that was really his name) was usually less likely to be spotted than the mountain lions that called these places home.

Bjorn lent a hand, getting the Humvee winch hooked onto a nearby tree. After a few moments, Rob's vehicle came unstuck. Grateful, he invited Bjorn and his friend to a local restaurant down the mountain. Doubtful he would actually show but figuring it worth the chance to learn more about this seemingly mythical figure, they showed up at the appropriate time and place. The military-grade vehicle, very protective German shepherd dog still in back, was already in the parking lot.

One could only imagine the loyalty and tenacity of that canine. It seemed entirely possible he was Rob's only family, maybe the one being, other than his employer, who actually ever knew of his whereabouts or existence.

Rob was quick-witted and friendly, and he enjoyed the best of food and drink. He shared a bit of his military background, was quick with a laugh, and was generous in return for the help given earlier in the day. Bjorn and his pal, who barely had two nickels to rub together at that time, were wined and dined like kings, all on Rob's dime.

Eventually, as the night wore to a close, Bjorn asked, with a bit of liquid courage, "What the hell were you gonna do if you didn't get that thing unstuck up there?"

With no delay or even a hint of kidding, Rob answered. "Sometimes, you just die."

The *life* in such a statement, the beauty, the simplicity, cannot be denied. It is not to say that one goes careening willy-nilly into their dreams. No, that is not the point. Listening to Rob's words, I hear that life is meant to be lived to the fullest and to be lived on your own terms—no one else's. Done so, there can be no regrets. The words of the Scottish revolutionary, William Wallace, have echoed down through the past seven centuries to become familiar to us today from the movie *Braveheart*: "Every man dies. Not every man really lives."

* * *

The two-mile or so walk to the campground had been intoxicating to my soul. Reinvigorating. This was a challenge worth taking on. I was certain of it once again. Many months prior, in the comfort of my one-bedroom apartment, finding myself on the Yukon River Quest website, I had been inspired. I was inspired now even more; I was exactly where I was supposed to be. This place, this river, and eventually, this race and I were to be one. No matter the outcome, walking to the cabin/office to check in, I knew that the uncertainty no longer scared me as it had for the first time a few hours earlier. It now fueled me.

The inside of the rustic two-room cabin that served as an office for the campground was perfect. Flyers of all there was to do in Whitehorse and the surrounding area would provide good reading, once I got my site and tent set up. An old drip coffee machine, a sign reading "Free Coffee" next to it, strengthened the feeling of friendliness here.

"How can I help you?"

The pleasant voice of the older lady was just what I would have expected.

"Steve Cannon, from Iowa. I had called a couple times inquiring about tent sites…"

"Oh, yeah. Here for the river race, from Iowa. I remember you. Let's get you set up right down by the creek that runs through the campground. A beautiful little space with a nice wooden footbridge you'll like. If you need anything, got any questions, stop up anytime. Good luck."

Sometimes you just die, Rob had said. Yep, that's how it is. Walking back toward Site #17, I'd never felt more alive.

This is the life I was meant to live, I thought. *When the lights do go out, I'll exit, grateful for the journey and with a smile.*

Chapter 32

RAINDROPS WOKE ME GENTLY; THEIR PERCUSSION AS THEY HIT the rain tarp covering the tent had no rhythm, yet it was somehow the perfect melody to wake up to. Unseasonably chilly and wet weather was no matter to me. The welcoming rays of the sun, strong winds tugging at the tent stakes—they too were perfect. I was inside a tent, set up just a few dozen paces from the lovely footbridge that spanned the crystal-clear running waters beneath. *When things are good inside, they are good outside.*

The lack of total darkness in the Yukon had little effect on my sleeping. Needing to get up to pee in the middle of the night, I found the fact that there was a bit of light still hanging around, eliminating the need for the headlamp, made the journey cross camp just another cool new experience.

It was time to fire up the stove, boil some water, try out the freeze-dried huevos rancheros, and brew some hot tea for the walk back into town. A date with Carl, Rob, and the river was today's only real plan. We were to meet at Kanoe People around noon. An organized paddle was leaving not long after, with a shuttle to pick us all up downriver. Oh yeah, and there was the grizzly bear clinic at seven in the evening. Hopefully nothing learned there would prove necessary, but just being in a place that offered "grizz" clinics was freaking great. I wasn't gonna pass up that opportunity.

Freeze-dried meals have come a long way. Recently, returning from a summer backpacking hut-to-hut trip in the Rockies, I thought, *This stuff is better than I eat at home.* I'm guessing the view from the deck of Betty Bear cabin, overlooking the peaks of the Rockies, some still covered in snow, had something to do with the perceived yumminess. Huevos rancheros in a pouch taste better looking out of a warm and dry tent in the Yukon than they do on the back porch of a one-bedroom apartment in the center of Des Moines.

Hot tea in hand, I threw a few supplies in my day pack; jacket, paddling gloves, stocking cap, and some energy bars would do for today's trip. Not far down the trail leading back into town was a nearly doubled-over pine with what I would best describe as a "tree house" some thirty feet up. I'd given it a twice-over when I'd passed it the day before, but I was in a hurry, excited to get to camp. So I'd done some homework with a few locals hanging out in the campground the night prior before I hit the sack.

The "tree house" was a nest and had not always been only thirty feet off the ground. The tall, proud pine had once been much taller, succumbing to the home-building of the mighty bald eagles, bit by bit, year by year. Eventually, unable to sustain the mass of the structure, the tree became what I looked upon, bent over to near ninety degrees.

If a nest was successful, meaning baby eagles hatched, the male and female returned every year, adding on to their home until the tree can no longer support the nest. The one I was looking at was the real deal. I thought, *My entire tent could fit into this thing!* I was told that the eagles added up to a foot in both height and depth each year's nesting period. Elsewhere in this area, a nest nearly ten feet in diameter and weighing over two thousand pounds had been found. Wondering if the tree house was an active nest or one that had outgrown its tree, I found my own perch, a nice trailside boulder, to hang out on, sipping my hot rooibos tea. The morning's rain, now subsided, had left a chill in the air. The tea was a welcome partner, warming both my hands and heart.

Hearing the loud screech, I instinctively swung my head back and over my left shoulder. I couldn't be sure what it was because I had never heard the noise before, other than on some wildlife TV show perhaps, but it came from somewhere high above. Before I could locate the source, another sound, slightly different in pitch, came from right above me. Shifting my gaze to the nest, I saw her—or perhaps him, as I have since learned males and females share the responsibilities of nest building and protecting of eggs and young eaglets. Whatever the case, I had a front row seat to an active nest. Events happened quickly. It must have been chow time, because immediately after the adult eagles called and responded, three little heads popped into view in the nest. I can only guess the communications taking place across the Yukon sky signaled, "I'm bringing home the bacon," followed by "Table's set. Thank goodness, these kids are driving me crazy!"

Sipping my tea in awe, I sat. The eagle had a wingspan easily ten feet in width. It dropped down from the heavens, clutching a fish in its talons, and nearly disappeared into the nest. Perched on my rock, I was close enough to the edge of the nest that from time to time I could see the young birds competing for the food. Eventually, the activity above slowed. I'm guessing after the large meal, naps were needed by all.

Chapter 33

THERE WERE PLENTY OF NEW FACES. ARRIVING AT KANOE PEOPLE at the designated time to take a prerace paddle down the river, my emotions were varied: I felt excitement, uncertainty, a bit of fear, and some more excitement. There were closer to a dozen folks there. Rob and Carl were in attendance, of course; the others I did not know, but one had a certain look to him—a look that hinted who the man might be. Older certainly, but old? Certainly not. He was seemingly as wide and thick as he was tall, which is to say he looked like the type of fellow not easily moved. There was both a harshness and a gentle quality to the man. Soon after I arrived, my suspicions were confirmed. He was "The Austrian," sixty-five-year-old Heinz Rodinger. If there was a legend in the field, from what I had learned leading up to the race, this guy was it. A stud in his younger days, he had competed at the highest levels, and since then had been competing, paddling, and adventuring all over the world. When he talked, much like the old E.F. Hutton commercials, everyone listened. He was not a braggadocious man but rather an ambassador, sharing when asked, offering advice kindly when he saw the need. He was easy to like and to admire.

I'd told Scott and the folks at Kanoe People the size of the kayak I'd trained in back home, so they were able to set me up with something similar. They mentioned at the time that perhaps a slightly longer craft, one that would "track" downstream a bit quicker, would be worth considering. My boat at home, a twelve-foot Current Designs Kestrel, was solid and comfortable, but *OK*, I thought, *consider it considered.*

After some brief instruction, we were assured that there was no hurry to get to the take-out point. "No one will be left behind. You could nearly coast the whole way and get there in a couple hours."

With that, we headed to the river to put in. Not wanting to be in front of anyone, I waited and watched. Carl and Rob shoved off close to last as well. We had decided earlier we'd head down river, the three of us all wary of our first go at the Yukon River.

WHAT THE HELL?!

Yep, I'd walked alongside the river to and from camp, but not right beside her. This water was moving, and moving freaking fast! I get that everything is about perspective. My perspective was a handful of Iowa, Wisconsin, and Michigan lakes—none of the "Great" ones either. Add in a couple of what now seemed interminably slow Iowa rivers, and the "uh-oh" factor was pretty damn high. I got no idea if uh-oh operates on a one-to-ten or a one-to-a-hundred rating. No matter. This sucker was at the high end of uh-oh.

My ego would not allow the words, "What the hell am I supposed to do with this?" to come out. I'm not kidding here. I had real fears of turning my boat upside down before I got three feet off shore. What my mind would not allow to be said, I'm sure my body language said for me. Somehow I got my shaky ass into that cockpit and the river—in what I can only imagine as a "We'll let ya slide this time" pass for the greenhorn from Iowa—and turned the nose downstream, with me somehow still upright.

I'd later come to find out that in our initial meeting, Carl and Rob had sized me up and decided that the tall, fit-looking fellow from Iowa was here to win. I'm sure, had they been paying attention to me as I entered the river, that those thoughts would most likely have been replaced with *Hope he don't die.*

I'll give Carl and Rob one thing: I was fit and not afraid to suffer. I had, in fact, gained a taste for it. Training in slow water necessitated paddling to get anywhere. If six hours of hard paddling were required, my body could deliver.

Scary as the fast-moving currents were at first, as I settled in, I realized they were of great benefit. *Shit, I'll coast all the way to Dawson City.*

Feeling so much better than I had fifteen minutes earlier, I dug deep for a few minutes to bring my kayak alongside my Jersey buddies' tandem kayak. Wanting to stretch themselves a bit, as Rob had come into the competition nursing a back injury, our chat was pleasant but short. They were off. I'd see them soon enough at the take-out designated by Kanoe People.

Not a single craft was behind me. It was perfect. I'd shoved off last, not only to avoid dumping in front of the masses but also for this right here. The Yukon River and the Yukon itself were mine. Both now presented themselves to be honored. Not often enough in this life am I in places where words, no matter how well I jive at the time of writing, do the place justice at all. It's my hope that my attempt here to describe the place to you sparks a desire to visit this place, or any number of wild places that lie in wait.

The kayak cut through the multicolored waters: turquoise green by the shore, blending into a deep, dark, yet somehow crystal-clear blue at its center. Looking behind me, an ever-widening vee stretched from the tail of the kayak, reaching toward the shore. Now well out of Whitehorse, expansive forest lined the great river, which turned, winding gently, revealing a new side of herself. Equal parts gentle and powerful, one felt safe within the forest's care on both sides. The next turn showed her strong, rugged, unforgiving side. Granite walls, rising directly up from her waters, were as old as the river herself. They held stories of all measure of high and low tides, of explorers and rushers who had come to this place. Some found riches; others, their demise. On occasion, mountains were visible in the distance. I imagined them as the grandfathers: the wise ones of this place, the gate-keepers and seers of all that happens here. From them, nothing could be hidden. I bowed my head from time to time, offering my respect to the forces at work in making such places. Greenhorn from Iowa though I might be, it was not lost on me that I was a guest in this place, and in all places, really. These forests, the thousands and millions of trees, the stone walls, the distant regal mountains, and the first sunny, clear sky, dotted with perfectly white clouds, would all be here long after my time was done. It felt right to acknowledge my smallness. A slice of humble pie I accepted with sincerest gratitude.

The quick-flowing waters, so daunting at first and then wel-comed for their forward-giving propulsion, were now proving to be a bit of a curse. In truth, it wasn't the water as much as time itself. The opening paddle was probably no more than ten kilo-meters, but its views, smells, and sounds were so intoxicating that were there no take-out pending I'd have stopped often, or even stolen a nap, just because.

I overshot the take-out anyway.

The current and I were still not one. Misjudging the left turn to shore earned me the need for some "bit in the mouth" paddling to get out of the stronger current and into the smoother waters that made exiting the river much easier. All the other paddlers made it downriver without incident. Endorphins were flowing in ev-eryone. Conversations were spirited. Standing there, in that place, among those people, I felt as if I belonged. I felt as if I had found my place, not just there in the Yukon but on a more profound level. Exhaling, emptying my lungs completely and holding for just a second before breathing back in, I allowed my lungs and my soul to fill as deeply as possible. It was a breath I wanted to remember. Forever.

Chapter 34

"One swat from a paw like this will do real damage."

Looking at the grizzly paw as she held it up for all to see, I thought, *Jesus, that thing is as big as my head.* Not only that, but the claws on it were menacing.

"Roll in a ball and try to remain calm if mauled."

Yeah. Good luck with that.

I heard what she was saying, but much like the advice to "stand your ground, look as big as you can, and make as much noise as possible if charged," this fell into the category of easy to say, damn near impossible to do.

I'd returned from the afternoon paddle with just enough time to gather my gear at Kanoe People and walk my way back into town for the free grizzly talk. How cool was it to be somewhere that had informational talks on grizzly bears and bear safety?

The display offered up a few cool items for us to check out. The giant paw with its ominous claws stole the show, and the grizzly hide covered an entire picnic table. Impressive. The speaker, not surprisingly, held bears and their surroundings in high regard, explaining that most confrontations were human error or because of encroachment on grizzlies' natural habitat. I appreciated her compassion for the animal and her reverence for the environment. Learning more about grizzlies was just another part of soaking in the Yukon, learning as much as possible about this magnificent place during what I knew would be an all-too-short stay. I could easily see and feel the allure that drew people to mountains.

I could imagine myself as one of those folks. Visions of the mountain men of the Rockies and memories of the amazing movie *Jeremiah Johnson* filled my head walking home late that afternoon. There was no doubt I was overmatched in this place, but how else do we grow if not by taking on the challenges, uncertain of their outcome? One of the great living mystics, Sadhguru Jaggi Vasudev, once said, "To those that are committed, there is no failure—just lessons learnt along the way." Yep, that's how I was gonna roll for the rest of my days.

Tomorrow was the prerace meeting and gear check in the afternoon. I'd decided in the morning to try out a kayak that was sleeker than I was used to, thinking perhaps my original choice, although quite stable, might be a bit slow. Although it felt a little like I was giving in to the devil on my shoulder, I convinced myself it wouldn't hurt to try.

Passing the eagle's nest, I saw no sign of activity. I paused for a bit, though, soaking in what had been a most wonderful day in the Yukon. The place was rubbing off on me quickly. Already, sentences were starting to end with the occasional "Eh?" With no action from the nest above, I headed on the short remaining distance to camp. Once again, dinner was served with a side of drizzle. The sun had shone brightly during most of the paddle that day, but that had been it. Continued rain and cold temps were in the extended forecast. Paddling a kayak for twenty-four hours straight or more in the rain would add additional challenges to an already monumental task. Too often, I was hearing the word "hypothermia," and veterans stressed, "Make sure you have plenty of layers and keep yourself as dry as possible. It gets cold out there, even when it's warm."

With freeze-dried lasagna refueling both my body and soul, I began to prepare for what I hoped would be another wonderful night's sleep. Cascading waters not far away provided a never-ending lullaby. Laying my head back onto the air-inflated camp pillow, its soft velour side up, I knew that life was sweet. My head settled nicely into the slightly deflated headrest. Somewhere, sometime, lost in my thoughts of the day, sleep came quickly. Rest was of the essence. The challenge was coming soon. It would be no small undertaking.

Chapter 35

In the morning, optimism and boundless joy were in shorter supply than they were the night before. The sun, like my soul, was battling to burn through the clouds, but they were legion. Occasionally, the clouds would obscure the light completely. But the sun was not gone. It still shone with the same intensity, but it could not be seen. Just now, I felt the same. My internal light burned no less bright as I worked through the morning oatmeal, my view from the tent vestibule as inspiring as each morning prior. Clouds had crept in as I slept, though. Clouds in the form of reality.

Swallowing the last few bites of breakfast required more water from the Nalgene bottle than previous breakfasts. *This is getting real, Steve.* Twenty-four hours from now, I'd be setting out to take the test. What if the Yukon River offered questions for which I hadn't prepared? It's the things you don't *know* that you don't know that can kill you. I'd read that somewhere—or else my subconscious was waxing poetic, sort of. Maybe this was the way a prizefighter feels before a fight or perhaps a soldier feels prior to the battle. You can never be totally sure of an adversary's capabilities. Experience is the only true teacher. Amassing facts gives you smarts, but not understanding. You can only truly know by doing. My overgrown beard, a couple of months in the making, provided a few minutes of distraction. Parts of each meal would attempt to seek shelter within the scruff. With no mirror to assist, I was my own mother gorilla, left to pick at the remaining oatmeal pieces hiding within. I'll leave it to your imagination as to whether, like a primate matriarch, I ate said leftovers.

Self-cleaning complete, it was time to break camp and get moving. I needed to get a quick paddle in a new boat done and then head to the mandatory prerace meeting. The voice in my head was shouting, *Never, ever try anything new on race day!* The other voice fired back, *Shut up! It's the day* before *race day.* This was no time for self-doubt or second-guessing. School was about to begin for real. Questions were soon to be asked. Answers would be demanded. For the first time, I paid no attention to the eagles' nest. There was no pause, no gaze at the horizon. If calls went out from the hungry eaglets above, they went unheard. A battle was being waged in my head. Many voices were competing to be heard. My ship seemed rudderless. The order sounded from within: *Dude! Center!*

Scott had the boat ready and waiting. All the crew at Kanoe People had been easy to deal with and interested in the needs of the racers. The additional length of the kayak they'd suggested for me was immediately noticeable. It was as if the craft I had been paddling had been put into the kayak-stretching machine overnight. She looked fast. Added speed also means less stability. How much less, I was here to find out. The quick-flowing waters had lost a bit of their "Oh, shit!" factor. Once in the river and pointed downstream, the boat cut through the water nicely; the sleek design of the seventeen-foot Current Designs Storm kayak had me tracking right on down the river. The longer boat also offered more storage. My left brain began to rejoice in the decision to try the new rig. The cockpit was narrower, and it pinched my hips a bit, but I hardly minded. Infatuated with the pace, I headed down the river. Each paddle stroke offered a greater return than I was used to. Stroke, stroke, stroke, stroke had been replaced by stroke, stroke, glide, stroke, stroke, glide. Math calculations were being done behind the scenes—so many fewer strokes per minute times sixty minutes times twenty-four hours. Yeah, that's a big number. I didn't need to know the answer exactly. Seventy-two hundred strokes per twenty-four hours of paddling. Apparently I did need to know.

It was a short paddle. I had my answer. This would be my weapon, the slight pain in my hips from the narrow cockpit be damned. I'd throw in some padding, make some sort of MacGyver modification, whatever it took.

Once I got back to Kanoe People, I shared everything I loved about this new rig and my concerns with the narrow cockpit. Boosting the seat up a little gave me some more comfort and made the kayak a bit more squirrelly—but just a bit. I decided I was good with it. It wasn't as cozy as my ol' girl from back home, nor her close relative I'd been paddling the past few days, but the perceived pluses outweighed the minuses. My decision had been made. I did my best to consider that item checked off the list.

Me, my new boat, and all the gear that would accompany me down the great river had a date at the Yukon Visitor Information Center. Registration, boat, and gear check had begun at ten and went until two thirty. That was the next stop. Well, the next stop after getting a quick *big* bite. My body and mind both were on alert and had been since arriving. Eating has always been a great joy for me. Somewhere deep down, I'm sure it is one of the driving forces behind my being an endurance athlete. I eat everything.

To this day, I remember my coach, sensing I was getting too caught up in all the "what to eat" questions while training and especially in the days leading up to a race, saying, "Dude, if it ain't nailed down to the floor, eat it."

Remembering stories I'd read of Ian Adamson stuffing his face with ice cream sandwiches and anything else he could get a hold of prior to some multiday adventure race, I thought, *I'm cool with that advice.* I dig awesome, fresh, healthy food—and lots of it. My metabolism is off the charts, but if I'm craving a pizza, deep-fried cheese curds, and a banana split, you can bet it's all going down. And you can be damn sure it ain't getting washed down with a diet soda.

It was quite a sight. People, boats, and gear were spread all over the place. Gear check was on. I could hardly believe it: my dream had become reality. I was here. Did I belong here? Well, I believe we all belong where we believe we belong. History is full of athletes, explorers, scientists, teachers, and parents from nondescript places who, from the outside, seemed to have no remarkable qualities. They all shared one quality though: belief. Belief that they belonged where they decided they belonged. No matter the thoughts or pressures of friends, family, or society, they decided how their story would someday read.

I stood over my boat, dry bags filled with clothes, food, a stove, matches, a bilge pump, energy bars, a water bladder, self-rescue gear, and an emergency blanket. I hoped the last two were unnecessary. On top of all that, there was my carbon paddle, water pump, spray skirt, waterproof gloves and socks, compass, sleeping bag, and tent. *Damn, that's a lot of gear to tote down the river,* I thought. Race directions made it clear this was a wilderness paddle and racers should not skimp on survival gear. Rescue, if needed, would not be immediate.

With my gear check complete, I headed inside to get signed in, receive my race bib, and have a seat alongside my fellow competitors in the auditorium for the prerace meeting.

Peter Coates, the race director, welcomed us all to the prerace meeting. The auditorium was packed to the gills with racers, volunteers, family, and friends. It was unlike any race environment I'd ever been a part of. Back home, I was considered an adventurer. The numerous ultra distance runs, twenty-four to thirty-six-hour adventure races, and all-day training adventures biking, running, and paddling I'd completed were not the norm in Iowa. We've since joked that there is a toughness that grows as one travels north. Iowa tough does not equate to Minnesota tough, which in turn gives way to Alaska tough. The harsher the region, the tougher the folks are that call those places home. Appearances are not everything, and I live by the simple rule that no man or woman deserves too much credit nor too little. Said another way, don't *ever* judge a book by its cover.

Sitting in that room, many of the race director's words went unheard as I took in my surroundings. In awe of it all, I couldn't escape the feeling of inadequacy. *For God's sake, there was a freaking Olympian here to race, and in Carl and Rob, two dudes who had taken on the damn Atlantic Ocean. Me? I'd paddled the Iowa River from Adel downstream to Des Moines.*

Again, the mental battle was on for control of my mind. The *We got this!* home team was presently getting the snot kicked out of it by the *What the hell are you thinking?* away team.

"Hypothermia. That's what gets racers here."

There was that word again. Peter's comment caught my ear and signaled a quick ceasefire in my head.

"It's unseasonably cool. Rain is in the forecast, so this year, more than most, staying dry will be the difference between finishing or not. Hypothermia is dangerous stuff..."

My mind had heard enough. *I get it already. It's wet and it's cold, and when night falls it will get much colder.*

Peter's words broke through again. "...and don't expect immediate rescue. It could be a day or more before we get word that you have dropped out and can get a rescue boat to you. Get dry, make food, boil water, and get in your sleeping bag. We'll be there as soon as we can."

I'd read all the briefings, articles, and blogs, as well as this excerpt from the race guide on hypothermia:

Hypothermia is by far the main reason that teams scratch and have to be rescued off the river. You may need two sets of spare clothes if it rains continuously. Put on warm clothes before you feel cold, especially a woolly hat. If you get shivery cold and can't paddle through it, stop, get out of the wind and rain, put on dry clothes, get into your sleeping bag and tent and make yourself a hot drink. If that is not enough to get you warm, fill a water bottle with hot water and put it inside your clothes. Warm up your core before worrying about cold hands and feet. A small backpacking stove weighs little and can save your race; that's why it's in your required gear list. Several monitor points and more formal checkpoints are spread out along the race route to help you as well... They will usually have a fire going and hot water. Take advantage of them if you get cold and cannot help yourself. Losing even a few hours getting warmed up will not disqualify you. Do not be an off-the-river rescue statistic. We want you to finish!

Lake Laberge was the other topic of much discussion. Not long into the race, this thirty-mile-or-so section claimed racers every year.

The point was again driven home by the race director, "One minute you're paddling calm waters, sun shining, and within minutes, a storm blows in, and calm, clear waters are replaced by nasty swells that dump even seasoned paddlers."

Rules were in place to keep racers within a couple hundred meters from shore throughout the lake, for their own safety. A colder, rainier spring meant colder water temps. Not the sort of place one wanted to go for a prolonged swim, trying to get body and boat to shore.

None of Peter's words came as a surprise, but it's one thing to train for a race like this and quite another to actually point your kayak downriver for the first time. We all gotta be a rookie sometime. I had no delusions. I knew there was much I didn't know. Experience is always the best teacher. A failing grade in this test held more consequence than anything I'd ever attempted, though. That was a fact.

Slides were clicked through, comments and advice accompanying each. Final instructions and encouragements were given as the meeting came to an end.

"We'll see you on Main Street tomorrow for the race start. Have a great evening and get some rest."

Like any Old West gunfight worth its weight in lead, the race start was set for high noon the next day. We were told to assemble downtown for prerace activities after staging our boats along the riverbank. The race start would resemble land runs from days past: all of us, at the gun, would be running the quarter mile or so through downtown in order to reach our boats and launch. First to the boats, first on the water. That was a chunk of real estate that held no importance to me. I'd be content hitting the water tenth, twentieth, or dead last. I had no delusions of grandeur. One goal: finish. Eat before hungry, drink before thirsty, parcel out effort conservatively, and above all, stay dry.

The cool drizzle, present for most of the day, accompanied me all the way back to camp. It was more a nuisance than anything, but the sun, now completely obscured, was forecast to be an infrequent visitor throughout the race. Belly full—a double serving of freeze-dried lasagna had done the trick—my best guess was that it was nearing eight in the evening, but I couldn't be sure. Leaving the prerace meeting, I decided the sun no longer served me. Camp traffic would wake me early as it had every day since arriving. My goal now was to connect as deeply with the river and the Yukon as possible. I'd come to this place, yes, to attempt the Race to the Midnight Sun, but I'd come even more to connect with this place and, in turn, myself.

Zipping the vestibule closed and resting my head on the pillow, I closed my eyes. I felt some trepidation, validating the quality of the upcoming challenge, but I also felt contentment. All we can do in this life, if really living is the goal, is dream big, prepare to the best of our abilities, and enjoy the ride. No doubt I was taking a big swing—my biggest. Just how big? I was about to find out.

The O.K. Corral? High noon? Yep. I'll be there.

Chapter 36

OPENING THE TENT TO GREET THE MORNING, FLAPS FALLING TO the side as the zipper arced bottom-left to bottom-right, I confirmed what my ears already knew: rain. It was of no consequence. My mood could not be dampened. Today was *the* day. Life seldom takes place exactly as we hope or envision. I'd made peace with that fact some time ago. One who is fully alive sees beauty in all situations, not just those that work out as they had hoped. *Perfect.* That was the thought breathing in the crisp fresh Yukon air. Game day had finally arrived. Having to throw on rain pants and a jacket now meant I wouldn't have to deal with doing so later. One less thing to worry about. Two people, looking out the same tent, seeing the same thing, can have completely different perspectives. I'd have been no more or less happy were it clear blue skies, sunny, and toasty warm. This was a wild place. Its unpredictability was its beauty.

I'd drawn bib #5 for the race, which meant I was first up that morning at eight thirty for final boat check on the river. All gear was packed away in the appropriate "dry bag" (waterproof bags designed to keep everything dry even if they dumped into the lake). These bags come in all sizes. Some are larger for extra clothes, while others vary in size to hold food, maps, and the like. What a sight! Canoes, kayaks, and Voyageur canoes (think Viking boats) for the team competition were lined up all along the riverbank. There were too many to count. Looking at the giant Voyageur canoes, I thought, *That would be a hoot, taking this sucker on with a bunch of your friends.*

I located my rig and began loading her with all my gear. Everything had its place. Food, drink, maps, and self-rescue gear in case I capsized—hopefully unnecessary!—stayed topside on the deck. Bungee-like straps attached to the kayak both in front and behind me made storing such things pretty easy. Rear and front hatches provided ample storage for extra food (probably way too many peanut butter-banana-honey sandwiches) and Clif Bars, along with energy drink powder and two extra complete sets of dry race clothing. An extra couple of stocking caps, pairs of wool socks, and gloves also were stored away. It is said in endurance racing you carry your insecurities with you. Which is to say, the less experience you have, the more eventualities you prepare for, even to the point of overkill. Boat fully loaded, I laughed, thinking I was somewhere between racer—some of the solo kayaks looked way less loaded than mine—and Beverly Hillbilly. *And we loaded up the kayak and paddled to Dawson City!* In my head, I sang the intro from the TV show I'd enjoyed as a kid so many years ago: "Come and listen to my story about a man named Jed…A poor mountaineer, barely kept his family fed…"

"Looks like you're ready to go!" a volunteer checking boats said, pulling me from my walk down memory lane.

"Man, I hope so. This shit is gettin' real."

We laughed.

Looking over the kayak, making sure all was legit, the volunteer said, "She's looking good. You're gonna do great. Keep yourself dry out there, and you'll be fine. Safe travels—you're good to go. We'll see you in Dawson City!"

As he walked away, I just stood there. The feeling was hard to explain. The crisp, cool breeze funneling down the river and the continuing drizzle didn't matter. An emptiness fell over me. At that moment I was seemingly everything and nothing. I was totally present. Were it not for the rain gear, spray skirt around my waist, and bearded face, I could have been one of the high-reaching pines, a wooden beam holding up the gazebo not far away, or any other inanimate object within view. In that moment, and for a few continuing moments, all universal hierarchy drifted away. I was no larger or smaller, no greater or lesser than anything or anyone. I was a part of it all, and I realized that without any one of them, this experience would be less than what it was. Only a very few times prior had I ever felt so connected, so a part of the whole.

Chapter 37

Stepping away and heading to the start area downtown, I felt a sense of accomplishment. I'd come to this place seeking both to lose myself and find myself, to connect more deeply with the real, unencumbered by the noise of everyday life. Amidst the excitement, energy, and apprehension, I also felt a deep peace and gratitude.

Not long after arriving downtown, Rob and Carl, my new buddies from Jersey, showed up. "You ready, mate?"

"I am."

One by one, two by two, slowly at first but eventually building to a steady stream flooding the street, we gathered. All of us from around the globe, in search of something or someone, had come to this place: Main Street, Whitehorse, Yukon Territory.

To be in the presence of so many seekers was such an honor. The energy of the collective echoed through us all. If an instrument existed that was capable of measuring such energy, like a seismograph of adventurous souls, this gathering undoubtedly would have had the device swinging violently. Each face, each body, was unique. Some would be pegged as athletes the moment they walked into the room; others, perhaps not. Male, female, tall, short—no matter. What lay inside the cover of each of these books was what mattered. These people burned bright and bonfire hot inside.

All of us had decided at some point that life was not meant to be lived lukewarm and that a life lived safely was wasted.

Chapter 38

THE TIME HAD COME. FROM THAT FIRST TRIP TO THE BOUNDARY Waters with Uncle Bob so many years ago, through nearly throwing my potential away for good, to finding *life*—every adventure, every training session, physical and mental, every bit of wanderlust, every desire to expand my self-imposed definition of possible...all of this had led me here. I stood among my peers.

This was it: the start of the world's longest kayak race, the Race to the Midnight Sun. The Yukon River Quest start was imminent. My mind was blank; my focus was sharp. I was totally alive. Was nothing registering, or was everything registering? This state of complete immersion into the *now* is what draws me to these places. The bullshit of everyday life is forced to disappear. This is not the place of voicemail, email, or snail mail. It is not the place of the nine-to-five, of water-cooler talk or reality TV. This is the place of quickened heartbeats. As your adrenaline surges, your senses are brought to bear, creating a heightened sense of all things. Focus and intensity live here. It's a place of simplicity and single-mindedness, or even a sort of no-mindedness. Words were being spoken. Somewhere they registered, but their meaning couldn't find its way into my stream of consciousness. No more words, instruction, or "go get ems" were needed. The task was at hand: the teacher had ordered that books be put away, and the test was now placed squarely in front of me.

BANG! The gunshot rang out, piercing through my senses and the dreary Yukon sky simultaneously.

Snapped into the moment, the cheering of the crowds, cowbells clanging, and horns blowing signaled that indeed the game was on. The surge of adrenaline sent some sprinting down the main stretch of Whitehorse, which was not quite wide enough to contain us all. Some, hoping to get to the boats before all others, hopped onto the sidewalks in an attempt to get around the slower, or at least less aggressive, paddlers. In no hurry myself, I took in as much of the grandeur as possible. Winning or losing, coming in eighteenth place, or DNFing had nothing to do with how quickly I made my run for the river. I knew there was no rush. Besides, there's a reason no one runs the 100-meter dash in a kayak spray skirt.

The jaunt was not long, maybe a couple of kilometers. Arriving at the shore, I saw my trusty kayak waiting. I imagined her like a horse, still tied to the hitching post as others galloped away, giving me that *What the hell we waiting for?* look. *Untie me, and let's go!* We had not spent much time together.

My old nag, safely back home in the stable, would have known better. We knew each other's tendencies well, having spent hundreds of hours together. She knew my motor was slow to warm, but that given time, many hours later, we'd open up. We weren't the sexiest on the water, and flashy pedal-to-the-metal accelerations were not our thing, but often times, many of those hot rods lay at the side of the road five or ten hours later, overheated or out of gas. I wondered if this new horse would be good with all that. We'd chatted quite a bit during our training runs the past week, but to say I really knew her would be untrue.

Trust is earned over time, a commodity we were not afforded. I'd decided early on not to go through the exercise of shipping my kayak to the north, a decision I never got totally comfortable with. Settling into the new kayak and freeing the paddle from its strap,

I sealed myself in. Securing the spray skirt membrane around the outer edges of the cockpit, I was essentially now locked inside, the lower half of my body and gear safe from the elements. The swift current caught the nose quickly. I settled the paddle back left, and the kayak snapped nicely downstream. Happy not to be bucked off, I patted the boat on the side, letting her know I appreciated her and that we were in this together. Every kayak and canoe was spread out in front of me; I paddled with ease—the current of the Yukon River doing much of the work—and soaked in the energy of it all. The locals sent us away just as they had welcomed us. Cowbells rang out, and there were cheers, applause, and well wishes aplenty from the shoreline. I did my best to acknowledge them all, hoping they felt my gratitude for their taking me in as one of their own and sending me off the same.

One kilometer down, 714 to go. I wondered what lie in wait.

Chapter 39

FAMILIAR? YES. BORING? DEFINITELY NOT. THERE WAS NOWHERE that the grandeur of the Yukon did not impress. You could stand anywhere in Whitehorse proper, and all you had to do was just look around. There was majesty in the hills and mountains rising up in all directions. I'd paddled this early section three times over the past few days. Each time, something new caught my eye. It was no different now, except for the fact that no one was waiting ten or twenty kilometers down river to fetch me out and drive me back to Whitehorse. This trip was a one-way deal. The energy accompanying that realization changed the game all by itself.

The plan was simple: "Let the race come to you" would be my mantra. Which is to say, take it easy, let the body stay warm, and keep the mind quiet. The biggest challenge going long distances is always the mind. Harness it, treat it kindly, and rock it to sleep. Call on it if need be, but it serves little purpose out there. Its job is to keep us safe, reminding us of danger and of the long, long miles remaining. None of this serves someone in the endurance world. The endurance world is a place of no mind. It is where we allow our body and soul to express themselves most fully. Mind chatter serves only to detract at worst and distract at best. I've found this to be applicable in everyday life as well.

Beauty surrounded me. The water below, shockingly cold, occasionally splashing onto my face from an errant paddle stroke, was a beautiful mix of blue and green. Giant stands of pines populated the foothills bordering the river. In spots, harshness was revealed. Immense rock formations showed through, and mountains rose in the distance. The Earth's majesty exposed my insignificance. I was a speck, less than a speck, on this landscape. My place on the food chain here was uncertain, but I knew I was far from the top. An odd sense of euphoria and fear was present. It was hard to discount that in this beautiful, rugged place, Mother Nature need merely flick her finger, and that would be all she wrote for me. How in the hell people who settled in this place survived was beyond comprehension. They had a toughness, a resiliency, that I would most likely never understand. Goosebumps, accompanied by hairs standing at attention on the back of my neck, would be frequent companions on this journey. The Yukon and her river were slowly revealing themselves. Few had ever made this journey or seen what I was now seeing. With each bend of the river, my love and respect for her grew.

Chapter 40

Before me was a fork in the road, or in this case the river, with the infamous Lake Laberge looming just a kilometer or two beyond it.

Holy shit! That ain't no lake, that's a freaking ocean! I thought.

Left or right? Damn it. I didn't remember any talk or mention of options to enter the lake.

Left or right, dude?!

The river was moving me along, and coming to a stop to ponder the answer was not an option.

"Left or right?! Decide! NOW!"

Left it would be. The water became shallow and slowed soon after. My fifty-fifty call had been wrong. I was straying more and more to the left. Continuing in this direction would not be an option. It was made clear all boats must enter Lake Laberge within shouting distance (a quarter mile or so from shore) for their own safety. It seemed obvious now that right would have been the proper call, but at the time it seemed two sides of the same coin. I'd figured the two paths would reunite, dumping me safely into the lake at the correct area. Now, a couple hundred meters off course, paddling had become a waste of time. Too shallow and mostly filled with tall grasses, I was stuck in a marsh. Dead end. The good news was I could see where I should be, not too far to my right. The bad news was there was no retreat. The flow of the river would make that much too arduous.

Walking the Yukon River had not been part of my pregame plan, but that's what it was gonna take to get me back on track. Testing the "floor" with my paddle, it seemed like walking would work. Soaking wet shoes that would remain soaking wet did not sound appealing. I'd packed a heavy set of wool over-socks, more like wool moccasins, just in case. This was not one of the just-in-case situations I had envisioned, however. Looking back, going barefoot would have been a better call, but unsure of the floor beneath me, the thought of rocks cutting up my feet led to the decision to get out of my shoes and into the knee-high, heavy wool socks.

Releasing my spray skirt and getting out of my shoes and into the socks were of little problem. Rolling up my pants, easing out of the cockpit so as not to tip her over, I stepped into the water. It took no time at all for the water to sink her teeth into me, through and over the top of the wool socks.

"WOW!" I shouted, the cold taking a bit of my breath away, "That's freaking *cold!*" I felt an equal mix of exhilaration and laughter. "Hello, Yukon River. I'm Steve Cannon, from Iowa. Nice to m-m-m-meet you."

Sure, pulling my kayak through the water hadn't been the plan, and, sure, having soaking wet feet and using my emergency socks hadn't been the plan, but I was all smiles, solidly immersed in the adventure. Attitude, in life and adventure, is everything. *Someday*, I thought, *this will make for a good story.* For now, a little walk, cold as it was, through the shallow waters of the Yukon River and Lake Laberge allowed for a deeper connection to this place.

Perhaps going left had been the right call after all.

Chapter 41

THE SHALLOWS ALLOWED FOR EASY REENTRY INTO THE KAYAK. Straddling the craft, one leg on each side of the cockpit, made it easy to keep the old girl balanced. Doing so in deeper water was not so easy. Once into the cockpit, legs still dangling off each side, I took a moment to get the wool socks off and wrung out. Temperatures were still in the upper forties or lower fifties. I figured the heavy wool socks, once back on and tucked down into the kayak, should keep my feet warm. Sealing the spray skirt made for a nice little "easy-bake body oven" below deck. Within a few hours, all would be back to normal. The little detour had cost me some time, but it was of no real consequence.

Entering the lake, back on course, I raised a hand to the race volunteer on shore, confirming I was within the required "safety zone." I scanned Lake Laberge ahead and the gray skies above; both looked a bit ominous, but they showed no signs for immediate concern. Every minute the lake remained quiet was a blessing. Blue skies, sun shining, and sights yet unseen during this adventure would have been more welcome. If Mother Nature held any ill will, the nondescript drabness of it all offered no clues to her plan or any chance of a warning. Only time would tell.

The currents slowed in the giant lake. A double whammy: it was arguably the most treacherous part of the race, and minus the river's swifter currents, there was no "free money." If you needed a rest, forward motion stopped, and Lake Laberge was not a place to hang out. If there was a time and place to take the bit firmly into your mouth and paddle like hell, this was it. Ranging between two and five kilometers wide, safety waited some fifty kilometers of paddling to the exit point of the lake. It felt as if I was on borrowed time. Fifty kilometers would take maybe five hours or so, but that 50K figure was deceiving. It was as the crow flies, point to point. Race rules prohibited crossing the lake in a straight line for our own safety. It was hard to say how much distance would be added by staying within yelling distance of shore. Sooner or later, a storm would whip up over the lake. That was not open for debate. Sometimes it would take hours, other times it would take a day or two, but it would come. Racing a clock that had no hands was tricky business.

Chapter 42

ORDERS WERE RELAYED FROM BRAIN TO INTERNAL STOKER: *Keep pouring the coals to her for the next five or six hours, boys! This is what you trained for…put these paddles to work and get your ass across this lake!*

My focus on form intensified, I began to work into an aggressive yet sustainable rhythm. Paddling, done properly, is not done with the arms, as you might think. Held at ninety degrees, the arms work as paddle holders, little more. Relying on arm power guarantees flaming out quickly. Inside the cockpit, my legs were braced firmly into the interior foot stops, legs slightly bent. Until this point, I'd paddled merely to supplement the existing speed the river graciously provided. With that gift now absent, I engaged my legs fully, locking myself firmly into the seat, so that energy could now be delivered throughout my entire body. Keeping the arms at or near ninety degrees creates a rotation where the core and back, stabilized by solid legs underneath, provide energy.

Big muscle groups all working to grab a full purchase of water, the paddle entered at ten o'clock on the left side. Devoid of seemingly any free propulsion now, there was a real sense of pulling the kayak through the water. The paddle exited about eight o'clock, which allowed for good balance, and I placed the opposite paddle at the ready at two o'clock. Leg pressure increased on the opposite side underneath as I prepared for the next stroke. Gently rotating my core, extending my body slightly, I engaged my core and back and pulled. Imagine a rope that is fifty kilometers long. Hand over hand, you pull yourself forward. Your journey is complete once you reach the end of the rope.

Cutting into the water and digging in with each stroke, the water of Lake Laberge dropping off the paddle with each exit, the difficulty of the task at hand had noticeably increased. However, so had the connection to the water below. Moving with maximum efficiency demanded it. A sharp focus was required. I couldn't be certain how long it took, but in time the focus, effort, and struggle became more of a dance, one in which my body, the craft, and the water became one. This didn't just include the water below me; the morning drizzle had become more of a rain. No matter. We were all connected. I was in the place that continued to draw me to these races and these adventures. I had crossed the threshold from the human's world—manufactured, loud, and fast—to the natural world, where all exists as one. Time no longer exists, and deadlines disappear. I was no more or less important than the giant rock structures that towered over me. From the pine tree, the loon, and the fish, surely going about its business below, to the drab clouds overhead—we were all one. It is in these places that I lose my man-made self. There is a saying I love: "One can be seen as intelligent by man or by nature, but never both." These places, these moments, taught me, and returning to them, I was reminded which master I wished to serve.

Like an unwanted visitor inquiring "Mind if I cut in?" just as you melt into your dance partner's arms, my dance with Lake Laberge was interrupted. The stormy giant had been sleeping nicely, allowing me and all who had begun passage earlier the smoothest of rides. But the increasing pace of the rain, previously beneath perception, was now a harbinger of changing tides. The flat, gray sky above had not shown any signs of

Mother Nature's changing intentions. A breeze now tickled the back of my neck as well. The glass top of the lake, a perfect reflection of all things above, was no longer smooth. Lake Laberge was coming alive.

Chapter 43

THE BREEZE, COMING FIRMLY FROM BEHIND AND PLEASANT AT first in that it provided a bit of an assist, was fool's gold. Any veteran of the race would have known that, for they would know that it came with a price. How steep the price, there was no way to know. Such was the diabolical nature of this section of the race. Once on the lake, there was nowhere to hide. No shelter, save one: getting the hell off it. Best case, I was three hours from that. Whatever the lake became the rest of the afternoon, I'd have to take it on. Heading ashore and waiting it out was not an option, as the race had time cuts. There was no certainty that any storm, if indeed that was what this was the start of, would pass soon. For the time being, Mother Nature's hand at my back provided a nice little push. I should have been more concerned, but as the saying goes, ignorance is bliss.

Boil a cup of water. How long does it take? A couple of minutes. A pot? A few more. A bathtub? Well, that's gonna take a while. Lake Laberge contains 107 cubic miles of water. That's one damn big bathtub, eh? The point is, you don't just stir something like that right up. You're gonna be putting the heat to it for quite a while before anything notable starts to happen. However, once something that size gets riled up, the power or chaos it delivers will be significant. And it ain't gonna settle down none too quick either. So often, a rainstorm, appearing quickly and dumping rain right from the start, dissipates as quickly as it appeared. Beware the storm that comes slowly in the distance, building moment by moment, for it is strong and stable.

* * *

I'd been fortunate to train a few days back home on Lake Red Rock, a large Iowa lake. It was a miniature version of where I now found myself. Lake Red Rock was the exit point for the Des Moines River. Fifty-five miles southeast of Des Moines, it had been a favorite training paddle. Red Rock could also whip up with a good wind, which Iowa has plenty of. Knowing of Laberge's reputation, I had intentionally placed myself into Red Rock during tough conditions. Thought it was scary at first, eventually the whitecaps became a place to play. I surfed the swells, using their power, riding them. *Free money!*

* * *

The buildup was gradual. Calm. Slight breeze. Water smooth. Slight swells. Drizzle. Now, rain. Still, it didn't matter. Far from it. There was no way to be certain, but this gift from the gods, as it seemed, was moving me across the lake at a quicker clip with less effort. Settling into the rhythm of it all—the breeze a constant—paddle, paddle, paddle, slight swell rising from behind…glide…*ahhhh.* I envisioned gentle wave after gentle wave releasing from a shoreline that was increasingly distant behind me. Each wave destined for me and sent with one purpose: to deliver me as quickly and with as little effort as possible to the lake's exit point, perhaps now less distance ahead then behind.

Paddle, paddle, paddle, paddle, swell lifting a bit more, sinking the paddle in just as it lifted the boat. A few quick digs, and I could surf the boat, maximizing the swell's gift and my glide. Returning a bit quicker now and with added height and intensity, my speed increased, and with all of these increases, an increase in focus was necessary. The longer, sleeker kayak was flying beneath me. Paddle, paddle, rise, glide, paddle, paddle, rise, glide. Paddle, paddle, riseglide. Paddle, paddleriseglide. Paddlepaddleriseglide.

The swells were quick now and perhaps three feet or more. I couldn't be certain, as the dance now consumed me totally. *No, I am sorry, you may not cut in. This is my girl!* I held her close.

It was the most perfect of dances. We were in total sync, sharing a perfect give and take. Time had disappeared. The swell would rise, I'd meet it with a sinking of the paddle, take two quick strokes, ride it, and glide. Perfect. Wild, untamed…"WAHOO!"

In an instant, however, it all came crashing down. With the suddenness of a record needle screeching across the vinyl, the music stopped. The time between that swell and the last was no different. Was it any higher or more intense in any way than the last? Had there been an increase beneath my perception? Had I leaned just a bit too far to catch the wave, crossing the unseen line beyond which there was no recovery?

Like waking from the perfect dream, unsure of what the hell was real or make believe, I had suddenly been thrown into a fight for my life. I was upside down in the Yukon River.

Chapter 44

"IF YOU'RE EVER SO UNFORTUNATE TO FIND YOURSELF DUMPED into a freezing cold body of water, I'm gonna ask you to try and remember, as all hell is breaking loose, the following: keep your freaking mouth closed!"

The class instructor had our attention.

It's a common misconception that in the situation I now found myself in, hypothermia is the killer. Many never get to find out. They die long before they can shiver to death. Instant immersion in damn cold water typically causes what is called "cold-shock response." Wanna play along? Go fill your tub with its coldest water and dump in a ten-pound bag of ice. Let it sit for a few minutes, then lower yourself in as quickly as possible. In response to your skin's rapid cooling, a sudden, nearly reflexive gasp for air occurs. Uncomfortable? Shocking? Hell yes! Now imagine that you had been forced completely under the water. Head and all. If that gasp happens, and you are unable to very quickly get above water, you die—drowned before hypothermia could ever get her icy hooks into you. I had not taken the challenge of the Yukon River Quest lightly. I'd read the glowing reviews about the race, which waxed at length about how tough, beautiful, and untouched the land was and how pure the task was too. Also, how dangerous it could be if things went to shit. Most don't plan on things going totally sideways, but some do. Had I not been one of those planners, I'd be dead.

I've enjoyed racing in some pretty gnarly events, mostly in damn cold conditions. Race directors warn without fail. "Don't show up with the price tags still on your gear." The message? All that fancy gear won't do you a bit of good if you haven't practiced with it enough. When you haven't slept in thirty-six hours, it's minus twenty degrees, the snow is blowing, and all your clothes are good and sweaty, you have a very limited amount of time to get your overlayers on, bivvy set up, stove taken out, and water boiling. These things seem pretty simple in the backyard with the warm breezes of summer caressing you on the back deck. I assure you it is much different in inclement conditions. I can remember having to think my way through just taking off my cycling helmet twenty hours into my first winter ultra. It was as if I was drunk. As slowly as you can imagine, I told myself, *OK, dude, reach up and pull down your balaclava, the clips are under that* after unsuccessfully trying to find the clips, fumbling around with my bulky mittens, which only hindered the process. *Now, unclip the helmet and lift it off your head.* It was as if I was instructing a three-year-old. I've since practiced, many times, in exact sequence, what to do the moment my pedals stop moving. I've grown wiser to the effects that cold, fatigue, and chaos bring.

Our local Iowa kayak company, CanoeSport Outfitters, offered instructional weekends each spring. Taking up the sport in earnest the prior year, the classes had been a big help. From basic paddling to self-rescue, they covered it all. It would have been easy to skip it that spring, figuring I've been there, done that. Again, had I skipped those weekends this year, I'd be dead.

Knowing the Yukon River Quest loomed, although it is not my nature to be overly detail-oriented, I had decided to take the weekend offerings again—specifically the self-rescue course. I was first in, last out. Need a volunteer? I'm in. Again, this was not usually my nature. Maybe somehow, some way, the universe knew what was waiting for me.

I listened with complete focus to the instructor, chest high in the lake, at my side. "Alright dude, here we go. I want you to rock the kayak side to side, take in a deep breath and flip yourself upside down. I'll give you thirty seconds or so to get free before I bring you back upright."

Oh boy! It's one thing to practice the techniques necessary to get out of your spray skirt in a foot of water when you're above water. This was putting your life in someone else's hands. Do I seem like I'm being overly dramatic?

Give it a try.

It felt much like being on belay when rock climbing. "Yeah, I know you got me, dude! I'll go for the hold when I'm good and goddamn ready!" Get ten feet or more off the deck, even safely on a solid rope being tended by someone who knows what they are doing, chances of danger nearly zero, and your mind will scream at you, *DON'T YOU DO IT!*

With practice comes confidence. Every failure brings us closer to success. Which, in essence, means there is no such thing as failure. If you step up to the plate—in anything—it's a win.

So I shut off the voice that had been trained since youth to keep me safe, rocked the boat, and entered a world previously unknown. And then I did it over and over again. Rock left, rock right, rock left, deep breath, and under I went. In warm waters, the deep breath just makes sense, right? You're going to be down there for a bit, so full lungs just make sense. In cold water—really cold water—it serves a second purpose. If it becomes instinct to grab a breath above water the moment dumping becomes inevitable, it may prevent that gasp taking place the moment you go under water and keep you from drowning, your boat now your coffin, your spray skirt still locking you in.

This raises the question: Is a spray skirt necessary? I suppose not one hundred percent, but in a race and a place like this, water in the boat, whether from paddle spray or rain above, means everything inside gets wet and cold. You store food and gear below the deck, so that's just not optimal. However, one could argue that going without a spray skirt is a better option than drowning.

A certain level of risk comes with these races; it's why we do them—to push, to challenge, to feel alive. Training and preparation minimize those risks. No way my epitaph is going to read, "Here lies Steve Cannon. He led a very long, very safe life." Ever wonder what your epitaph, your message to the world, will be?

The moment a kayak tips, spray skirt attached firmly around the cockpit, the water instantly pressurizes the spray skirt. You can pull with all your might, but no matter your strength, that spray skirt isn't coming off. No way, no how. It had been impressed on us more times than I can count during every class that if you do only one thing before setting out, make sure your spray skirt release handle (and the handle of every one you are with) is visible. If you or your companions take off in a hurry with that handle inadvertently beneath deck, it's game over if they tip. The only ways to get out depend on if they can right themselves—flip back up—which isn't easy, or they have a knife available topside and can cut their way out, or a fellow paddler saves them. Without that release strap, physics will win. Every time.

Chapter 45

IN A SECOND, PERHAPS LESS, I GASPED AS DEEPLY AS POSSIBLE, filling my lungs. Instinctively, I knew the point of balance had been crossed and there was no return. The boat was going over. I was going under. And just like that, my world was literally flipped upside down. Moments earlier, surfing the whitecaps of Lake Laberge, completely tuned in to the energy all around me, all was synced up. The intensifying weather had whipped the water into a frenzy beyond my skills.

Somehow—perhaps through training, perhaps by luck, or maybe via divine intervention, if you are one who believes in such things—I had dodged the first bullet. I had been able to control the gasp reflex. My lungs were full. Full of air!

Multiple clocks were now ticking. I had a minute or two to get free of the boat or I would drown. If I was able to free myself, then the second clock became important. I'd have between five and ten minutes in this water, and after that, my body would shut itself down to the point that I would be unable to self-rescue, get back into the boat, and get my soaking wet ass to shore and attempt to get warm. Every minute in the frigid waters of the Yukon would increasingly debilitate me. The body, in its effort to preserve vital organs, reduces blood flow to the extremities—hands and feet first, then legs and arms, if necessary. Getting to oxygen was imperative, obviously, but it far from guaranteed my survival.

Where is it? Why can't I feel it?! Frantically my hands reached out into the darkness. Left, right, more foreword, more backward, left, right, more to the side, less to the side… *Where is that strap? Why can't I find it?! Help! Someone please help me! I'm drowning! I don't want to die!*

My mind raced. I was in a full-blown panic, locked into my kayak, upside down in the Yukon River. There was no help anywhere near. Would this be it? Was this how my story was to end? My mother, who had given me love during times when I deserved none, who enjoyed my adventures vicariously but asked, only half-jokingly, not to be told of them until "after." How could I have done this to her? Dying in some distant place—no good-byes or apologies allowed—would be the ultimate welch on a debt I owed her for never giving up on me. Dying didn't scare me. I was grateful for having found this life after losing it for so long, for having some sense of self, and for being able to find my path—and more importantly, for having the stones to follow it. But to die in silence, unable to tell so many people how much I loved them and how much I cherished their friendship and support? That was unacceptable. Yet, it seemed my fate. Without my consent, Mother Nature and forces beyond my control had decided this was my time.

Unable to find the nylon strap that would free me from this predicament, which I had made certain was accessible, I accepted the inevitability of it all. *This is where it ends for me. Sometimes, you just die.* With perfect clarity and peace, those thoughts entered my consciousness. How long I had been without air, frantically struggling? I couldn't be sure. Time had been bent, distorted. Had panic made the time fly, or had it slowed time to a crawl? Were all the thoughts, seemingly rapid-fire as I struggled for life, desperately wanting to be free of this boat, taking place over just a few seconds, or had it been minutes? Any sense of time ended the moment I went head down.

I was going to die. Complete acceptance came, and with it, to my surprise, complete peace. I share this with you now so that you can move forward, so that you might loosen up just a bit, go for your dreams, and approach the edge knowing that the end, when it comes, is nothing to be feared. Death waits for us all, but I can tell you with absolute certainty it does so with loving, open arms. There's no pain, no sadness, just a welcoming hand leading you to the other side.

As quickly as it had arrived, it left—the panic, the flailing arms, the thoughts of a mind grasping for answers unavailable, all the noise, all the chaos. Stopped.

I'd read many accounts of adventure athletes, who in their attempts to achieve the previously unthinkable, had faced death and experienced a slowing of time, a clarity allowing split-second decisions to be made perfectly. Most of us have heard the phenomenon described as "The Zone," a place where one is able to block out absolutely everything other than the task and the moment at hand.

The intensity of my situation and the eventual acceptance of exactly what was going on produced a similar instant of clarity.

Open your eyes. These are not the murky, muddy waters of Iowa. Just open your eyes, grab the rip cord, and get yourself out of here. And with perfect calmness, as if all that had just transpired had never happened, I did just that.

Opening my eyes, there it was. How I had not felt it in all my frantic, albeit blind searching was hard to fathom. I can only imagine my rescuers finding me and wondering, *Why didn't he just let himself out?*

With the same calmness I'd had back home, practicing under the perfect safety and supervision of our class instructor, I simply reached my right hand forward, grasped the spray skirt's nylon release strap, and sunk my elbow into the skirt to decrease the pressure capsizing had caused. With a quick tug, the skirt, and I with it, came free.

Like a newborn leaving the calm and safety of the womb, I entered a harsh, cold, wild environment above the water. The peaceful moments spent in the "in between" world were gone. Short, violent gasps for air attempted to fill the void left by however the hell long I had been without it. Clinging onto the kayak, attempting to sort and process all that had just happened, it seemed the storm had intensified dramatically. Perhaps it was just in my head, but everything seemed wilder. The waves? Larger. The temperature? Obviously, colder. The wind? Whipping.

It took every bit of self-talk I had to calm myself down. Specific things needed to be done correctly and in due time. I was alive, but if I didn't get myself calmed down, panic would end me. One clock had been dispatched. I had not drowned. I was alive.

This was of no consequence to the second clock, however, still counting down. If I was not able to get the shaking, shivering, and ramblings of my mind quieted, death still waited.

Getting back into a kayak is a skill. Kicking my way to shore was not an option. It was too far, and the kayak was too heavy. Time and the cold waters would eventually incapacitate me. Leaving the kayak behind and swimming to shore was not an option, either. It held all my gear and clothes. Like it or not, I was still very much connected to the boat. My survival depended on getting back into her and paddling to shore. But the waves, now three feet high, maybe more, would make doing so nearly impossible.

Chapter 46

You're OK, you're OK...Calm down, breathe...Calm... down...breathe...

My breaths came short, quick, and uncontrolled at first, but slowly I was able to talk myself off the ledge. In an environment and situation beyond my control, getting myself under control was imperative. The rhythmic pounding of the waves, two or maybe three seconds apart, added to the challenge. My body began to accept the not-yet-numbing cold, and with that acceptance I was able to begin calming the mind. Certain things needed to take place in a certain sequence and in a timely fashion. My body, fine for now, was beginning to alert the extremities of their impending shutdown. Time was of the essence. First task: flip the kayak. Doing so would not be not easy, especially with a loaded kayak. Upside down or right-side up, they're not made to just easily tip over. Doing so would require going back under. The thought of returning to that place, sinking myself entirely again, was not well received. Like a child whining, "But mommy, I don't want too!" my mind revolted. I can understand how someone fighting the cold on some distant mountain could just relent. At the moment, my body, acclimated to the new environment, was comfortable. As comfortable as it could be. Holding on, hoping for help that probably would not arrive in time seemed a better option to going back down there. The mountain climber, stranded and exhausted, just wants to take a nap, just a little nap, for a respite from the struggle. They know, but are no longer willing to acknowledge, the inevitable result of doing so, and so they just go to sleep, never to wake—or they summon the will to keep moving, knowing they must.

It took a major pep talk for me to get going. Tick, tock, tick, tock, the clock continued to count down. This alarm offered no time out, no snooze button. When this clock stopped, without warning, I'd be done for.

Come on man, let's do this. We gotta get this boat upright.

I was two people: One just wanted to snuggle up in a ball and cling to the fleeting but existing "comfort," while the other knew what needed to be done and urged the other to get to it.

OK, OK, shit, shit—shit! Back under I went. The cold was somehow worse now. Water flooding back into the top of my jacket, my head totally under, I could feel the desire to gasp, and I resisted the urge with all I had.

Once below the boat, I mustered every bit of strength in me to not just flip the boat but to *lift* it and then flip. With no floor below to push off of, this meant a timed, breaststroke-like kick, followed by an immediate over-the-shoulders kayak press and flip. Every inch of lift mattered, as it would minimize the amount of water that would remain in the kayak.

The maneuver lasted mere seconds, but coming back above water, kayak upright, I felt exhausted. If I'd had ten dry matches before, I'd just burned most of them getting the boat flipped. Life was being sucked out of me. The cold waters of the Yukon River were my personal Dracula.

More self-talk, more deliberate breathing to calm my sporadic gasping. Tick, tock, tick, tock. Flipping the kayak, as miserable a task as it was, had required determination and strength. Getting back into the kayak required all that and more. Mounting the boat, balancing without tipping it back over, and getting into the cockpit without dumping myself and the boat back over would, in these conditions, be the equivalent of trying to ride a greased pig.

Chapter 47

THANK GOODNESS FOR MY PADDLE LEASH, WHICH TETHERED THE paddle to me. I had not always owned one. In these conditions, once capsized, I had been forced to let go of the paddle. How far it would have floated away during the struggle without that leash was anyone's guess. Again, training, the advice of seasoned paddlers, and listening to that advice saved my bacon. Self-rescue and getting back into a kayak is impossible without your paddle. The saying should not be "up a creek without a paddle." That dilemma can be reconciled. Rather, the saying should be "trying to get back in a boat without a paddle."

Much of my gear, especially the life-saving pieces, remained attached to the boat. Most important among them now was an item called a paddle float. For those of you with kids or who can remember back to your early days in the pool, think of "water wings," but for a paddle instead of your arms. In my current predicament, a couple of water wings for the arms would have been most welcome as well; I could feel my strength starting to wane.

The paddle float, once inflated, would allow me to lift myself out of the water, get my chest on top of the kayak deck, and slide back into the boat. Having a task to focus on was a great help in distracting my mind from the cold slowly taking over all my bodily functions. My training kicked in: get your breathing under control. Maintain complete focus. Grab the paddle float, unscrew the cap, take a few deep breaths, exhale into the float; it was ready. Sliding one end of the paddle into the float—this would be the end remaining in the water—I slid the other end of the paddle through the deck webbing. Again, I'd need to muster a good bit of strength to kick myself up. Using the paddle perpendicular to my body as a brace, I could push up and out of the water and lay chest-down on the kayak, facing the back of the boat. Once successfully there, I could then rotate my body 180 degrees and slide back into the cockpit.

I'd practiced this technique for hours. Eventually it became quite easy. Now, it was as if I was doing so after twelve beers. Everything needed twice the focus and unfortunately took twice the time. Was it the conditions, the lake rolling me around and tossing me like an old shirt in a washing machine? Was the cold really zapping me this quick? Both, I'm sure. Tick, tock, tick, tock. I needed to get off this lake.

Another hard kick, a push up from the paddle, and onto the kayak deck I went. My legs followed, exiting the water, swinging onto the deck, straddling the cockpit, and like that I was free of the lake; the split second of relief was followed by a slow-motion "No, no, noooo!" And over I went, back into the freezing waters of the lake. Either I had swung my legs up with too much force or a wave had caught us; maybe both. Whatever the cause, I was back in the water, my entire body rolling off the deck. I'd been out of the water a second, maybe two, before slipping back in. It may as well have been the first time, as it was just as shocking to the system. Again, gasping, my attempts to calm myself ensued. That had never happened in class or following practice sessions. Looking back, it would have been wise to practice in the nastiest of storms back home, not just in the calm, warm-water days of summer.

Again, once I'd calmed down a bit, I steadied for a second attempt. Tick, tock, tick, tock. Kick, push, up, steady…steady…no, no, no! And over I went, again. A third attempt. Kick, push…slower this time, which took more strength, but I needed to remain steady…go slow. I did my best, though I was more impaired than I was just minutes prior, to feel the boat and tune in to the lake's rhythm, realizing I was not leading this dance. Again on deck, I felt the boat rock beneath me, the waves continuing to move, raising and lowering the boat as I tried to steady her. I was finding the balance point, the line that could not be crossed. The problem was, the line wouldn't stay still. One moment it was here, the next there. Like a bucking bronco, the lake was seemingly trying to get me off balance in order to buck back the other direction, sending me back to the water. And again, just as I settled in, ready to begin backing into the cockpit, off I flew.

This time, there was no gasping for air, my head again above the surface. No, now there was only rage. I roared, cursing all things Yukon. This place, this race, these waters, this boat. To the heavens I cursed it all.

"WE HAD A DEAL!"

In reality, no such deal had been struck. No guarantee of safe passage had been made. No matter.

You can all go to hell! You go ahead and throw whatever you want at me! Is this all you got? I'm not gonna quit! I'm getting back in this boat, and I am going to finish this race! I don't need you! I don't need anyone!

I was twelve years old again, just being told of my parents' impending divorce, locked in the bathroom, wailing at the mirror. All alone, I had screamed for minutes on end. "Why, why, why? Why me?!" And in that moment, to my detriment for decades to come, I had decided, *To hell with people. To hell with everyone. I'm on my own.*

With that same anger and resolve, I cut ties with everything around me. Treading water, hanging from the kayak's side, I told myself, *No one is going to save you, no one is here to help; you're on your own.* With the same steely resolve of that hurt, lost kid so long ago, I decided I was getting back into that boat with this next effort. There would be no next after this next. With 100 percent certainty, I knew I would be successful. Don't ask me how I knew, because I can't explain it any more than I can explain the moment of peace and clarity that had allowed me to free myself from the kayak in the first place. No wind, wave, lack of balance, or waning strength would stop me. In that moment, I became master of my surroundings. I ruled the waves. I ruled the wind. Gravity was under my command. This kayak would throw me no more. I was getting back into this boat, NOW. I would have bet my life on it. I *was* betting my life on it.

Chapter 48

Tick, tock, tick, tock. Soon, there would be no "tock," and I had no way of knowing how many more seconds remained. What I could be certain of was there was more time behind me than in front of me. A problem I had not considered with starting so very conservatively was that very few, if any, boats were behind me. Had I placed myself further up in the pack, something I could certainly have done had I been more aggressive early on, there would have been safety in numbers. Were I to have witnessed such a calamity as I now found myself in, I would have offered assistance without hesitation. I'm certain fellow racers would have done the same, were any of them around. There just weren't. There is a mutual caring and respect for your fellow racer in the adventure sports, more so than in other sports I've done. The inherent dangers of paddling a river like the Yukon, facing down temperatures of minus twenty or lower during events like Arrowhead 135, Tuscobia, or Actif Epica, all of us there to race, made us also realize that if someone was in need, it could be appendage- or even life-saving to help a brother or sister out.

With a resolve unlike any other before or since, I prepared myself for what I was absolutely convinced was my last chance to right the ship and get my freezing ass to shore. With a frog kick from below, I raised myself up over the paddle lying perpendicular to the boat. Pushing up from the paddle, I swung myself up into the deck once again. The storm continued to whip the lake more and more into a "washing machine gone wild" type of mess. The wave hit the boat again, just as it had without fail every couple seconds or so for the last many minutes. I was ready for her. When she zigged, I zagged. My strategy had been refined over the past failed attempts. Another wave hit; I leaned into her, counterbalancing so as not to be flipped over. I was making sure I could ride this sucker. I had been in too much of a rush before. To pull this off, I needed to time the lull perfectly, allowing a split second of calm that I could then take advantage of to back my way into the cockpit successfully. To speed up, a lesson I have since learned in harsh environments, I needed to slow down.

The lake and I continued our dance. Similar to a bronco being busted, it seemed with each wave that didn't dump me, things calmed a bit, if only in my mind.

Still topside, time slowing, completely focused, totally in tune with the lake's energy, I leaned into the swell, waited for just a moment for her power to pass, and as quickly and smoothly as possible I backed into the cockpit while simultaneously turning my body 180 degrees, from belly down to belly up—and just like that, I had done it. I was back in the kayak.

YES! YES, YES, YES!

Back in the boat, though, my relief, joy, and exhilaration once again were cut short.

Tick, tock, tick, tock.

I was happy that clock still ticked but realized also that I was not yet clear of danger. Had I not gotten back in the boat, without someone coming by—a racer or a support person, both highly unlikely—I would have frozen to death in that lake. Now in the boat, death by freezing was still a possibility, but less so. If I could make it to shore—which I could now surely do—strip out of all these wet clothes and into dry ones, and get my body temperature back to normal, I would most likely survive the ordeal. Continuing the race was not even a thought. Survival was all that mattered. Nothing else.

Chapter 49

It was like sitting in a cold puddle. Not surprisingly, I'd been unable to get the fully loaded kayak high enough out of the water in flipping it over to empty it of all the water it had taken on. The shock was minimal, since I was entirely soaked. Nonetheless, I was sick of being cold and wet.

Removing the paddle from the deck webbing, I turned the boat to the right, making straight for the shore. The waves, still relentless, were insatiable in their appetite. Fortunately, the water in the boat provided some added ballast. I'm unsure I could have kept it upright to shore without the unintended assistance the extra weight provided.

Tick, tock, tick, tock.

My strength was beginning to fade; the delay from thought to execution was growing. The cold and wet were winning. My senses and physical abilities were losing. Each paddle stroke required an order sent from head to arms, its arrival more Pony Express than Wi-Fi. A couple hundred meters to shore should take a few minutes, tops. Especially if one was freezing cold and in a hurry—which I most assuredly was. Sometimes in dreams I try to run, being chased by some kind of bogeyman, and fear grips me in such a way that my legs are frozen. It felt like that. My brain screamed *Go, go, go! Get to shore, man!* and was completely perplexed why the body would not—in this case, *could* not—respond. I was trapped in a body, its batteries blinking red: "Recharge necessary."

Tick, tock, tick, tock.

Keep your eyes open, man. No sleeping…no! Don't you do it! Paddle, paddle…

My mind begged, pleaded, and ordered my body not to check out. I'd caught myself nodding off a few times, the time between my brain sending the paddle order and my arms hearing the order being too long. I kept snapping to, like a driver headed down the highway who's been too long behind the wheel, only to nod off again moments later. My time was nearly up.

Had I continued paddling half-conscious? Had the current or some other divine source pushed me the last fifty meters or so? I don't know. The sound of the kayak hull against the gravelly shoreline snapped me awake with the suddenness of the alarm you hate but continue to use because, well, it works. Gathering what was left of my senses, realizing I had made shore, I rallied all my resources.

Get out of this boat, get your clothes off, get your dry clothes on…NOW! the drill sergeant inside barked, desperate to see this through.

A burst of adrenaline provided the necessary focus to heed the orders. Nearly falling into the lake, legs wobbling from all that had happened, I popped the rear hull compartment, grabbed the dry bag that held all my back-up clothing. The strong wind, as cold as the Wicked Witch of the North, was a blessing. Stripped naked on the shore, the cold air was like a slap in the face, its harshness buying me some time. Somehow, humor found me.

Naked, running in place as I started grabbing dry clothes in an attempt to begin raising my body temperature, I busted into my best Chris Farley rendition of "Maniac" from the movie *Tommy Boy.* Laughing, as it does in all things, helped.

What a sight I must have been. I imagined a grizzly, lurking not far off, his hot meal having just washed ashore, thinking, "I want nothing to do with that, whatever *that* is," and sauntering disappointedly away, deciding something so crazy could not possibly be good for the belly.

It was as if I was instructing a two-year-old how to dress. *Stocking cap first…good. Now long underwear…bottom first, then top…No no no, are you not listening? Bottom…oh, what the hell. OK, top first. Let's go. Pay attention, we ain't got all day.* Every item of clothing had to be ordered, and it took all my focus to accomplish what normally would be mundane tasks, doable without a second thought.

Chapter 50

TERRA FIRMA. DRY LAND. EVEN AS MY STRUGGLES TO DRESS CONtinued, for the first time since finding myself upside down, I had a sense of safety. Dry land—something we all take for granted—was now a luxury, a treat I had longed for during the past ten minutes or so. The work of warming the body remained, but at least for now, out of the water, drowning was off the menu. That was nice.

I wonder if anyone has ever shivered a tooth out of their head? The fact that sarcasm, unlike most of the heat, had not left my body was a good sign.

Finally, fully dressed with every single layer on—pants, jacket, coat, stocking cap, gloves, and shoes—it was time for the "heat dance" to begin. Not unlike the First Nations people before me praying for rain or sun, my prayer dance intention was for warmth. Jumping jacks, sprints up and down the shoreline, push-ups, skipping, and high knees accompanied with all manner of incantations defined my dance for life.

The ticking of the hypothermia clock, so quick and loud moments before, began to slow and soften. Feeling began to return to my furthermost extremities, followed by a slowly detectable warming of my limbs and eventually my core. It had taken many minutes on that Yukon shoreline to bring all systems back online, but I had done it. My thoughts were clearer, and my body was able to respond to them in a near-normal timely fashion. Noticing a large piece of deadfall just behind me, I decided a quick sit to gather my thoughts in order.

I was alive. And with that realization, my head fell into my mittened hands. I began crying uncontrollably, the events that just transpired overwhelming me completely.

Chapter 51

HOLY HELL. NOW WHAT?! WITH THE SAME STUNNING REALITY the frigid waters of the Yukon provided earlier, the thought of what to do next hit me.

Crickets. No reply. For the moment, sanity restored, body temperature at or nearing normal, the reality of things had resurfaced. "What next?" was a simple question, yet it was one my mind was unready or unwilling to take on. Happy to be alive, free from the watery tomb the kayak had nearly provided, my mind was content to bask in its dry, cozy inner Shangri-La.

You can imagine the inner dialogue. Fresh from the experience of the past fifteen minutes and a *Titanic*-worthy sob-fest, I was just simply incapable of answering my own questions.

The initial hurdle was the cause for denial. Potential answers, all being bandied about subliminally, began with having to get back in the kayak and resulted in me thinking, *No freaking way I'm even considering that question.*

Tick, tock, tick, tock. The race clock never stops. Race or no race, there was no getting away from the reality now confronting me. I either gave up the race, or I got back in the boat, which in turn meant getting back into the water, which was even angrier now, as if somehow mad it had let one get away. Like the opposing army in *Dances with Wolves* as Kevin Costner rode his buckskin horse Cisco across the lines of fire, Lake Laberge taunted me. *Hop back in that kayak. Try that again and see how it works out for ya.* I wanted no part of that challenge.

To decline meant quitting the race. After all that had transpired, who would blame me? There would be no dishonor. The problem with this dilemma was that I had not come to this place to assuage nor impress anyone. I was here to find out what I was capable of, to see where my limits lay and press past them into the unknown. I had now come to that junction—yes, in a much different way than I would have hoped or imagined, but nonetheless I was there. Rescue would come at some point. It could be hours, but it would more likely be the next day. That option was no more palatable.

Ultra racers are great liars. To quell the inner demons that often surface, it becomes necessary to tell a whopper or two, like the once-again-in-trouble husband who has staggered home, two drinks past his limit and many hours late, promising "Honey, just don't hit me with the frying pan, and I'll never do it again!" Those of us out in the night, pushing past the edge, tell our own whoppers to ourselves. Those lies are told with the intent merely to shut the mind up long enough to regain positive thought, eventually getting us so far into the event where anything short of a finish becomes unacceptable.

At the next checkpoint, I'll quit. Just shut up till then. Or, *This is the last time I ever do one of these stupid events...but I have to finish. Then that's it. I promise.*

Sometimes, as was the case that I now found myself in, the next task must be accepted with zero commitment to anything further.

One step, that's all I'm asking. This request, so simple, is met with no resistance. Repeated enough times, your personal challenge can also be overcome. With a mile to go in your first 5K, seemingly impossible, one step at a time eventually becomes reality.

A decision was reached. I'd get back in the kayak and give it a go. Much bargaining had been necessary.

I ain't putting that spray skirt back on. If I even start to feel that boat tip, we are headed back to shore. And it was definitely "we." There were many voices being heard. Many were none too polite, contradicting, speaking over one another, demanding an audience.

Finishing the race is not even an option. If we get through this lake, victory can be declared. Then we are done!

You get back in that boat, and you're an idiot.

Go ahead, hop on in, but next checkpoint, fire, or any other sign of civilization, and we are out of here. To which I, whoever "I" was, agreed.

Hopping back on the horse seems like pretty good advice unless you're the dude that just went flying, taking a header off the back of a now-gloating bronco. Nothing before or since has scared me like getting back in that kayak. Every survival instinct told me not to. This, however, was the moment: the reason I had come. We do not always get to choose the timing of such moments in our life. In adventures like these, it was even less likely that we'd get to choose such things on our own terms.

Like a cowboy having just been sent flying for the umpteenth time by a yet-to-be-broken bronc, with everyone outside the corral saying, "Enough is enough, another day," I rose from the piece of deadfall where I had been sitting, ignored their pleas, shook off what dust I could, and took the necessary steps to saddle back up. Could I go the distance? There was no way of knowing. I didn't care. I only knew I had to get back on that horse.

Chapter 52

SURVIVAL INSTINCTS SUGGESTED—STRONGLY SUGGESTED—THAT I not stray far from shore. That seemed like prudent advice. The dilemma was twofold, however. To get off this lake, which was now the bane of my existence, in the shortest amount of time meant not hugging the shoreline. "As the crow flies" made geographical sense, but the shoreline meandered back and forth, in and out. Remaining close to the right-hand shore, comforting as the thought seemed, also meant a steady stream of left hooks would be forthcoming. The storm, which had whipped the lake into a mega-sized kayak-eater, had not yet subsided, and nor had the turbulent waters that had followed.

If I was to have any chance of getting through this portion of the race, I'd have to shut off the survival part of my brain, ignore its pleas to play it safe, paddle straight back into the angry waters, and once I was far enough from shore, bank right and attempt to again ride the waves that had dumped me. There was no other way. I tried. The swells were just too strong, and their continuous crashing treated me like a human bobber, the swells determined to push me back onto shore. It had been a necessary exercise to attempt the strategy of staying close to the shore. I needed to prove to all the dissenting voices in my head that this plan was not only unwise but also impossible. It was the only way to rally the troops to paddle straight back into the teeth of the beast.

I let the currents carry the boat the few feet back into shore, resigned, knowing that this would not work. Stepping back out of the kayak, onto shore, the boat was pulled out and turned, 180 degrees, facing directly back into the lake. With the tail of the kayak still just enough on shore to keep it steady, taking a few deep breaths, and straddling the craft, I walked forward, lowering back into the cockpit.

I'd have to paddle straight into the oncoming waves until I was clear of the shore, which would be no easy task physically. Never mind the effort to ignore the voices in my mind screaming, *What the hell do you think you're doing?!*

Once sufficiently clear of shore, I'd be able to swing right, clear of the point where the shoreline jutted out, and have another go at riding out the storm and reaching the exit from the lake, still ten to fifteen kilometers away. With each stroke, I left the safety of the shore behind. With each stroke, the demons in my head became fainter.

I remember an interview with Danny Way, a skateboarder of the highest degree who jumped the Great Wall of China on his board. In Steven Kotler's amazing book *The Rise of Superman*, when Way was asked "Why do you do it?" his answer was "Because the edge is the one place ghosts can't follow." I understood with perfect clarity.

My concentration was once again focused on the task at hand. Now clear of the point, I timed my right turn perfectly, swinging the boat at just the right moment, the lake picking me up and propelling me in the direction of its exit. There was a sudden peace to things. The lake now held me firmly, safely in her grasp. Perhaps I had passed some sort of cosmic test. Perhaps it was a test given to all who attempt to cross, with her handing out the final grade, deciding who shall and shall not pass.

I was back in the game, out again on the edge, where the ghosts could not follow.

Chapter 53

I HAD STOOD AT THE GATE. ONE STEP WAS ALL THAT HAD SEPA-
rated me from the other side. I had not cowered from it. It was
not as I had imagined. I had thought it would be chaotic, with
me kicking and screaming, pleading for just a bit more time. No,
it was much the opposite: warm, peaceful, and welcoming, like
the most wonderful bear hug from a long-lost friend. Returning
from that place, I was left to wonder what beauty lie in wait just
one step further. Time would tell, but I would not be unlocking
that mystery today. There was a sense of relief in knowing that,
but also an odd sense that I was missing out.

Much as I had decided during my final attempt to get back
in my boat during my self-rescue, determinedly decreeing that
I would tip no more, the kayak and I now were solidly in rhythm
with the lake's movements. Happy to let her lead this part of the
dance, I surrendered, accepted my place, and in doing so learned
an invaluable lesson. Fighting the current can be done, perhaps
with some success, but eventually we all tip over. The current
always wins. Be aware of it, trust in it, use its energy, and enjoy
the ride.

Now, "enjoy" in my current situation would be a stretch, but
there was still nowhere else in the world I would have rather
been at that moment. Sure, if I could have been in that same
place with my backup gear still below deck and dry, instead of
on my body, that would have been preferable. But I was all in.
Every piece of backup clothing I had brought for the journey was

being employed. The rain continued. The day was growing long in the tooth. This meant temperatures would be dropping even lower. If I was fortunate enough to clear the remaining portion of Lake Laberge, which was seeming more and more likely, a very long, cold, increasingly damp night on the Yukon River would be my reward.

Chapter 54

A new Prometheus, chained upon the rock,
  Still grasping in his hand the fire of Jove,
It does not hear the cry, nor heed the shock,
  But hails the mariner with words of love.

"Sail on!" it says, "sail on, ye stately ships!
  And with your floating bridge the ocean span;
Be mine to guard this light from all eclipse,
  Be yours to bring man nearer unto man!

—"The Lighthouse," HENRY WADSWORTH LONGFELLOW

THE MONOTONY OF ENDLESS HOURS ON THE LAKE, WAVES NOW subsided, body and mind numbed into a half sleep, was interrupted by the flicker not far in the distance. There were no lighthouses to signal safety in these parts, but the campfire in the distance provided what I imagined to be a similar comfort.

I remembered back to the advice given at the prerace meeting: be prepared; the lake is nearly fifty kilometers long and can take fast teams six or seven hours, and it can take slower teams eight to ten. Waves can grow to six feet.

My sense of time, along with other senses my body deemed a waste of available energy, had been discarded, leaving me unable to make any sort of educated guess at how long I'd dwelled in the beast's belly. It was safe to bet that it had been double-digit hours. The waves at their most unruly—well, like all warriors, I am probably prone to exaggerate their size due to ego or perhaps the fear they had struck in me. Six feet? No. Head high as the kayak and I descended to the low point, awaiting the next sweeping upward? For sure. I'd later hear that the prior year's solo champion went ass over elbows seven times on the lake in the same storm that almost overtook me before finally abandoning the race. At the time, I did wonder how many others, if any, had been taken out by the great Lake Laberge. It would have made me feel better to have not been the only one. I'm not sure what that says about me...or perhaps I just don't want to admit what that says about me.

Hours earlier, I had been holding on by a thread, all systems shut down other than those necessary to keep forward progress possible. But the campfire, still farther in the distance than I liked, but gradually closing, began bringing those systems back online. It had been necessary to shut off the mind completely, for it only reminded me of things like time and distance, both killers of the spirit. Now, the flames allowed a thawing of that cold determination.

So many hours prior, letting myself believe I'd finish crossing the lake would have been an invitation for unaffordable disappointment. Believing that the exit loomed just around the next point would have resulted in despair, were it to turn out not to be so. So I planned on each summit being false. Typically, I'd use each upcoming landmark as a carrot: a reason to hope, but not to believe. I had dedicated myself to reaching the lake's end. No more or less.

A stranger's voice, the warmth of a campfire, an opportunity to let down my guard. I didn't know which would feel better, but I didn't care. The small light off the front of my craft signaled to them as their fire had done to me. I could only imagine the stories they had heard, the comfort they had provided to all those before me. A few quick, deliberate strokes guaranteed my landing onto the rocky shore. Words of welcome and encouragement felt surreal. A volunteer far from home, there enduring the cold wet storm—a savior indeed—steadied my kayak as I slowly came to rise out of the cockpit, trying to keep from falling on my face, legs suffering from inadequate blood flow from being in the same position for so many hours.

That feeling. Familiar. I allowed myself to soak it in. It was not a mirage or some hallucinogenic moment brought on by the turmoil and exhaustion; this was the real thing. The warmth of the flames reached out to caress the exposed skin of my face and in doing so brought both joy and relief. I received a handshake, kind words, and a hug from a stranger. The hug was perhaps in an effort to arrest what may have seemed like an impending face-plant exiting the kayak. But that didn't matter; it warmed me on the inside.

Lake Laberge had handed me an entire race's worth of drama. More than I could have hoped for. It had provided such a challenge, I had discarded any thoughts of completing the length of the race the moment my kayak's underside had shown itself to the menacing clouds above. Warming myself by the fire and in the cozy company of others, the old question arose again: *Now what?*

Chapter 55

"HOW'S THE RACE TREATING YOU SO FAR? TOUGH CONDITIONS out there, eh?"

I thought to myself, *Dude, you have no idea.*

But the volunteer did have an idea. Not only had he been braving the elements, exposed to the rains and wind with no real physical activity to warm himself, he had also heard the tales of each racer passing before me, a fact I had forgotten easily, as I was completely oblivious to anything outside my own pending battle. The 2006 Yukon River Quest was claiming its stake. It was my toughest quest to date.

Sea legs, I thought, still forming a response to the volunteer's query. The question perhaps had already been answered based on my appearance. I could only hazard a guess. As I continued to contemplate an answer, the need to relieve myself took precedence over any sort of response. Heeding nature's call in a kayak, as you might imagine, was no easy task. Most societal rules did not apply in these places. However, it seemed polite to take a little walk from the fire and eyes of volunteers to enjoy what would be the spiritual experience of emptying my bladder. Once adequately clear of the instinctively proper "no-pee zone," I found just the right tree to prop a hand against while leaning slightly forward. This was going to take a while. Not only did the tall, sturdy tree provide stability to a weary body, but my outstretched arm could also play pillow, my head resting momentarily atop it. The thought had occurred to me maybe an hour prior to just pee my pants. Why not? Already damp head to toe, why suffer any further discomfort? The initial warmth of such action held some appeal. Thankfully, I had chosen the option I now very much enjoyed.

Nearing the end of the physically and emotionally fulfilling experience, the reality of my surroundings struck me. Dogs, bees, and even attending the state fair have a higher chance of killing you than being mauled by a grizzly. Those facts, however accurate, brought little solace in the middle of grizzly country, the blazing fire on the shore and the voices of volunteers now a bit too far away for comfort. My newfound comfort and commune with nature suddenly seemed less soothing. The bogeyman was never actually under my bed, nor anyone else's that I ever knew, but alone in the dark, the mere possibility of his presence took on more probability in that place. Now fully certain that the eyes of a mama grizzly, thoroughly frustrated with my unannounced visit and her patience at an end, were upon me, I made my return to shore with more haste than my exit minutes before.

Returning to the safety of others, there was little time to dally. Checkpoints are the ultimate double-edged sword. Providing necessary support—be it logistic, nutritional, or even emotional—they also, if you overindulge in any of the above, are the perfect trap, where racers convince themselves that they have nothing left to prove. The proposition of heading back "out there" grew more daunting each moment I let the heat of the flickering fire ease my spirits. Its message was intoxicating: "You are safe here now. There is no need to leave. Warm yourself. Enjoy your richly deserved comforts."

Somewhere, beyond where thought registers consciously, my decision had already been made. I'd be pressing on, staying only a few moments to drink, eat, and be merry. It had been a more-than-necessary stop, but its job now done, it needed to be left behind. The next chapter needed to be written. After a hearty handshake that became a hug and a "Thank you so very much for being here," I began making preparations to shove off into the unknown.

It struck me as I paddled away that I never did answer the man's question: "Tough conditions out there, eh?"

Chapter 56

Lower 30 Mile, the section I now entered, marked the lake's end and so much more. It meant shelter from the winds and, more importantly, shelter from the waves the winds created on the lake. Safely back onto the Yukon River, I could feel the wilderness offering shelter on both sides, and the narrower waters felt much more immune to the effects of said wind. The entirety of the lake dumping back into the river also meant a reintroduction to fast-moving currents and occasional sections of riffles or mini-rapids. All were most welcome. After endless hours crossing a lake, which prior to the storm had offered little to no assistance and made each stroke necessary to continue forward movement, reentering the river offered free money. The opportunity to coast when needed, still propelled forward by the natural movement of the water below, was a gift from the northern gods.

One hundred kilometers now lay behind me. The time of night, or perhaps morning, was unknown; I could only be sure it was not yet two in the morning. Had it been, I'd have been removed from the race for missing the time cutoff.

Carmacks, the unofficial halfway at the 325-kilometer point and a mandatory seven-hour stop, was not even on my radar yet. That was a bridge too far. I had bargained with my inner demons to release me until the end of the lake, agreeing we could open up deliberations again then. There was no way they'd sign on for another 225 kilometers. But how do you eat an elephant? One bite at a time. My plan was simple: I'd continue to bargain like a kid desperately clinging to the controls of his Xbox—"Just a few more minutes, then I'll be done!" I would make goals so small that to my brain they would be no real cause for alarm, letting me continue on. Were it even to catch a hint that I had plans on Carmacks or even the Little Salmon, the next major checkpoint 150 kilometers down river, I'd be facing a full-on revolt: a "You put that paddle down, now!" command, in my best pissed-off, fed-up parent voice.

For the time being, all was OK. There was no need for any high-level negotiations. The swift currents had me moving nicely, and I was still in the middle of a very long mental and physical sigh of relief. Being alive and off that lake was more than enough for now. I could be looking at as many as fifteen hours to Carmacks, a distance at that moment so mentally unacceptable that taking a couple of hours to paddle, breathe, and reestablish some sense of equilibrium seemed a good idea—one that was acceptable to all parties.

Chapter 57

ADVENTURE HAS THE ABILITY TO PROFOUNDLY EXPAND ALL things, good and bad: the highs are higher, and the lows are lower.

With the ordeal that was Lake Laberge now hours in the rearview, paddling down the river had become a battle with monotony, winding left then right then right then left. Once you have spent a couple of hours on the sharp end of the stick, struggling for your life, the comedown leaves everything else a bit wanting. It was not that the Yukon River had suddenly become void of all its amazing attributes. From the outside, had someone tuned in to "Steve TV," the environment and situation would have seemed most intriguing, I'm sure.

For the past two or three hours, I'd been experiencing one very prolonged exhale. Transitioning from *Holy hell, what just happened?* to *Holy hell, it's a long way to Carmacks,* suddenly I found myself feeling desperately alone.

Typically, this is one of the main reasons to take on these challenges, if not *the* reason. At some point, if the challenge is a worthy one, we will be forced to face ourselves. The undertaking eventually strips away all the distractions we have come to accept as real, as an integral part of ourselves: our job, our family, our email, the dogs, the cats, the six o'clock news. Perhaps these all are a part of who we are and the life we have designed, but they are all superficial constructs, many times keeping us distracted from our true identity and potential. Meditation is a gradual undressing, a homecoming, returning us to our original self if we stay in the game long enough.

For me, an event like the Yukon River Quest provides the same experience. Neither promise happy-go-lucky, whistle-while-you-work comfort from start to finish. Both take guts. Life provides ample shiny toys to distract us for a lifetime. Digging deep, going within, and facing our inner demons gets messy, but no one I have ever met has regretted taking that path. This is not to say that the family, friends, job, and Wolfie the dog must be kicked to the curb in favor of these challenges. It is to say that they will all be that much more cherished and enjoyed as one pursues the best version of oneself. Unfortunately, I was now smack-dab in the middle of the darkness, both physically and metaphorically. It is a weird thing to be certain that there is nowhere else on the planet you would rather be and nowhere else on the planet you would rather *not* be at the same time. This was exactly why I had come to this place, this moment, to see how I would handle it. How does the saying go? Be careful what you wish for?

It is not an easy place to access. Sit down to meditate. Find a place of comfort and ease, take a few deep breaths. It's wonderful...at first. Sit a bit longer, and the voices will start. The mind will put out endless thoughts as diversions, roadblocks, safety barriers, and guardians of the chaos. To pass through, to sit and face the music, takes real courage, but if you sit long enough, stay in the race long enough, you enter a space of ease and peace: the outside unchanged, the inside transformed.

In training as well as in racing, when this moment presents itself, I try to remind myself that this is why I came, that the journey to this place was not easy. Do not back off now. Hold on for all I'm worth. Knowing the effort required to get here, I want to take full advantage of the opportunity, for if I cower, if I relent, comfort awaits—but great effort will be required to return and to pass this test again.

I have not always been successful, but every time I have been able to punch through, whether it be in a quiet space with candles lit and incense burning, seemingly serene except for the battling voices in my head, or in a kayak, soaked to the bone, wanting for nothing more than sleep and a warming fire, the rewards have always been worthy of the effort.

The Yukon River had stripped me bare. Alone and lonely, I knew that if I could hold on just a bit longer, the sun would shine again. No dark time lasts forever.

Chapter 58

"Any port in a storm. Any light in the darkness."

A single drop of water. What can it really do? It cannot even do as much as bring the smallest of flowers from the dirt. The dust on the porch furniture will not cower from it. No stream will flow faster to the river because of it. But many drops, falling over and over again, possess the power to form the grandest of canyons, drive a person to the brink of insanity, or, for me in the river, soak me right to the center of my bones.

The rain and the dark of night had been relentless, though not as much in their intensity as in their seeming endlessness. And then the darkness began to wane and the rain started to subside. With all of my being I had held onto one thought: *Just make it through the night.* I had scratched and clawed, the dirt of the Yukon under every fingernail, hoping to hold on just a bit longer—and then again just a bit longer after that. One more moment only *really* matters to the person suddenly face-to-face with their mortality. A hint of light, just the possibility of it, was all you wish for when you're consumed by darkness. The rain stopping seemed an aberration; its constant *drip-drip-drip* had been a companion for so long.

The long, wet night was being forced to relent by the promise of a new day. A glimmer of hope—not to finish, as such thoughts were still too heavy to take on, but to continue—took the place of the dreariness that had been the norm for much of the evening.

Geographically, I wasn't sure of my exact location. It mattered little. I'd held on just long enough to see the dawn of a new day. There was victory in that.

Chapter 59

"We'll probably pull over soon. Not sure we have time to sleep and make the time cutoff, but if we don't, there's no way we'll make it."

Sleep. Damn. It sounded so inviting. I hadn't allowed myself even the thought of it. For one thing, like the father of the father-and-son canoe team I had recently paddled up and began talking to, I wasn't sure I could afford the time. Or perhaps I could. My sleeping bag and inflatable pillow, safely inside their dry bag, were the only items remaining on board that weren't damp. Their promise of warmth and comfort were as much a curse as a blessing. I'd been awake going on thirty hours, and I had been wet for most of that time. The option of pulling off-river, boiling some water, and perhaps making a cup of tea was so enticing. The problem? I was scared that once I was in that sleeping bag, my tarp strung up, protected from the elements, I might opt out of the race entirely and just decide to homestead.

The father and son and I shared a bit more chit-chat. I was envious of the son, probably in his mid-twenties. What an adventure he was sharing with his father! They would have a lifetime of stories by the end of the race. Would that be Dawson City, the true finish line? Or perhaps sooner? It didn't matter really, not in the grand scheme of things. Wishing them well, I chose to paddle away. There were reasons to stay. The invite had been made. Strength in numbers, companionship, warmth, sleep, getting out of the damn kayak and feeling circulation in my legs: all these beckoned. Paddling away was not easy, nor was I certain it was the best course of action. Time and miles would tell.

Damn it! Why didn't I listen to a couple of the old-timers? A few had mentioned they'd be taking along a large pizza for sustenance. Thinking I was already quite the adventurer, knowing more than I really did, I had declined to do so. At that moment, choking down my fourteenth peanut butter-banana-honey sandwich, I again wondered why.

A pizza would have taken up all of about a foot of storage. And at that moment, had you paddled up alongside my craft with one, you'd have been able to name your price. One of my fingers? Not sure why you would want that, but I tell you what, you could have had two of them if you'd add another slice to the deal! It took an inordinate amount of water to wash that damn sandwich down. A pep talk was required to swallow each bite. I became my own mother: "Open up the hanger, here comes the airplane…Chew chew chew, make the airplane go away!" Writing this is actually firing up my gag reflex. I was learning a valuable lesson in food diversification on big adventures—and learning it the hard way.

Since I left the Yukon to this day, I have yet to eat another peanut butter-banana-honey sandwich.

"Hey there!"

I snapped alert, pleased to see the voice was real and not another mirage; a handful of boats were stopped along the shore just ahead and to the right. It was not a checkpoint, but that was fine. I was getting out of this boat *now*.

One of my fellow racers was kind enough to help me get the kayak beached and steadied as I wobbled out, looking anything but graceful. My legs had been in the same position for hours. It was all I could do not to fall into the chilly river water as my legs struggled to sustain my weight, devoid of their normal strength and balance. A few chuckles accompanied my exit. They weren't laughing at me; rather, they were commiserating, letting me know that they'd been there, done that.

I asked what was up, and they explained that there was a homesteader's cabin here, which I had failed to notice earlier due to my enthusiasm at finding boats and humans around the bend. All of the racers were in different states and stages: some seemed untouched by the elements and surroundings, perfectly at home. *I bet they all have pizza*, I muttered internally. The rest, if I'm being honest with myself, still all seemed to be in better spirits and physical shape than I was. Hopefully a quick break from the arduous task at hand would provide some levity: physically, mentally, and most importantly, spiritually.

Making sure the boat was firmly ashore, I took a walk up the well-worn trail leading some fifty meters from river to cabin. It was as simple as a structure could be: four walls, a desk, and a chair. Nothing else. A primitive outhouse stood another twenty paces or so farther up the trail. These cabins, I found out from those who were familiar with the region, were remnants from the gold rush days. Most, I was told, were all rotted out; time and the elements had beaten them down. This one, however, was home to a fellow whom I would have loved to meet, and although I never would, he continues to inspire me to this day. As I learned during my respite that day, a week or two before things began to freeze up each year, the old man would paddle downstream to this place, spending the long, hard winters of the Yukon alone, armed only with enough provisions to survive the winter, pencil, paper, and his thoughts.

I sat in his chair, my hands resting on top of his desk, facing the wall. I imagined myself writing in the dimming light of an oil-fueled lamp, though this was long before knowing I would ever write anything for public consumption. I imagined what it would be like to be that alone for that long. I was reminded of an article I'd read about a man from my home state of Iowa who travelled each year to Yellowstone to live in and oversee the most remote of camps. He told of the struggles each year: how the solitude, at first blissful and a relief, would turn to near-despair as his mind screamed for interaction and the peace, almost bliss, that awaited on the other side. Sitting there, I promised myself I would someday experience something similar and put myself in a position to get to know myself on a deeper level.

My last few minutes at the desk, I thought about what I might say to the man who made this place his home each winter. What would I ask? I lost myself in the hypothetical meeting, and I somehow felt some of the old-timer's wisdom, his spirit, finding a home inside me. Knowing yourself before you miss the time cutoff is life's greatest challenge.

Chapter 60

It was two hundred kilometers from the Lake Laberge checkpoint to the Little Salmon. I'd figured conservatively I could make that paddle in sixteen hours. That estimation was made safely in my nice warm tent, however, having just finished my third training run down the river under a mostly sunny sky. The current temperature was a comfy seventy-three degrees according to the bank clock I'd passed walking back to camp that day.

I pondered the conversion factors. I was wet through and through because the rain, although occasionally relenting to a drizzle, made drying anything impossible. I was sleep-deprived, underfed, and dehydrated, though I didn't know it at the time; my mind, annoyingly, would not shut up. It wanted answers. It wanted answers because it already knew the answer. I was two people or, more accurately, two minds. It is a difficult thing to explain, the battles fought within. The mind exists to monitor all things and to keep us safe. We are conditioned from before we are aware by well-meaning keepers, "Be careful of this. Be careful of that. Get down from there. What do you think you're doing up there?"

Were I to engage with those voices and take the bait my mind was offering, I knew where it would lead me. It sensed danger, discomfort, and unfamiliar territory. The initial question of how long it was to the Little Salmon was not the mind's endgame. As we continue to push our limits in business, adventure, and life, we become better and better at seeing past the trappings of our well-intentioned, play-it-safe mind. We realize that sweet fruits lay waiting beyond.

The question of "How long do you think it will take to get to the Little Salmon after all you have been through…in your current state?" was just an opener. To engage would mean looking into the future, leaving the moment. It would mean then facing the answer, which would be a larger number of hours than I could accept. From there, I'd find myself at the mercy of the inner conversation. I'd be no more able to shut it down than I could slow the currents of the river itself.

I knew where my mind wanted to go. It wanted to take me to a place where this perceived madness would end. It dangled the simple, seemingly innocuous question in front of me. I only needed to answer it, and all the chills, hunger, and aching joints could come to an end.

At that moment, the Yukon River was no longer my adversary. Perhaps it never really was. Perhaps it is always the mind, seeking to keep us safe in all things, that must be mastered. Maybe those who accomplish amazing feats do so not because of genetic blessings but because they push beyond the mind, realizing through trial and error—never failure—which are the real barriers and which are just perceived blockades.

I was farther out over my skis than I'd ever been in any adventure up to that point in my life. I steadied my mind with that very realization. It was natural that the mind would try to shut down this venture into the unknown. I thanked it for looking out for me and ended the conversation without allowing an answer to its original inquiry.

What are you doing? Get out of that boat. Get yourself inside. You're gonna freeze to death out there.

Nope. I don't think so.

I was back in the moment. Mind quieted for now, I paddled on. My destination? Farther down the river and further into the unknown.

Chapter 61

Nothing had changed in the external world. The tall pines, of the darkest and at the same time brightest green, still lined the crystal-clear, fast-running waters of the river. Winding without end, each bend was another turn of the page in the Book of Yukon. It had been a story I had immersed myself into for the past seven days, never tiring of its prose. Until now.

The lightweight carbon-fiber paddle eased into the water at about my two o'clock, found its purchase, and pulled past my body to exit the water near my five o'clock, just as it had thousands of times since yesterday. A few stray drops of the mighty river would occasionally find their way onto me as the paddle dug into the water, left side, ten o'clock. I was already wet from head to toe, so the drops were of little significance other than just being annoying.

Ever notice how when you are good and tired, the littlest inconveniences can seem monumental? I had passed that point somewhere not long after sunup. Now, if I were given even a bit of good news, it would most likely have been met with a generous dose of bah humbug. Ebenezer Scrooge had nothing on me at that moment.

Want to take a nap, Steve?

No.

Want to stay awake, Steve?

No.

How about some dry, warm clothes, Steve?

How about a nice big glass of SHUT THE HELL UP? How do you like that answer?!

And with that reply, the conversation between whoever now inhabited my brain and what remained of me came to an end. I was sputtering on fumes. Each paddle stroke now took concerted mental and physical effort. Although thankfully still upright, again it seemed my kayak was more coffin than craft. Every muscle ached from hours on end of being unable to change position. If it didn't hurt, it was because it had gone numb some time ago. Instinctively I had wondered if the sleeker craft would cause troubles hours downstream. The cockpit was a different fit from the boat I had trained all year in. "Never try something new on race day." It's not a rule. It's a law. Without fail, if you break it, you pay. Typically it refers to new socks, nutrition, or other race-type items. Why it doesn't specifically mention new bikes, running shoes, or kayaks is probably, and this is just a guess, because nobody would ever even consider doing something so dumb. The thought gave me a small chuckle, which was as rare an event over the past few hours as any glimpse of the sun had been.

I could have chosen a kayak nearly identical to my training boat for the race, and could I have gone back in time, I'd have done so and paid any amount asked. The aching in my hips was relentless. I was a sinking ship, hemorrhaging what little fight I had left into the waters of the Yukon River.

"UNCLE!" I screamed into the wild, hoping for some sense of relief, comedic or otherwise. "UNCLE!"

The race had me in the tightest of bear hugs. With each plea for mercy, air exiting my lungs, the kayak ignored my requests, seizing the opportunity to tighten its grasp. Were I flexible enough I'd have just collapsed forward onto the hull, letting the currents take me where they choose: downstream, ashore, anywhere.

Without discernible thought I reached forward, released the spray skirt, and shimmied my way back into the cockpit so as to free my legs from their confines, hanging each off their respective sides of the kayak.

Paddling stopped. Everything stopped. I was a shell sitting on another shell, neither with any life left in them. Scooting my butt a bit forward allowed me to recline just enough that my head could rest a bit, tilted back, life vest serving as a poor excuse for a pillow. For the first time in my life, I felt an understanding of how someone exhausted and cold could knowingly allow themselves to fall asleep, even when they knew they would most likely never wake. At that moment, anywhere would be a better place than the present…even if that place was nowhere.

Chapter 62

"I WANT TO GO TO A PLACE I HAVE NEVER GONE BEFORE."
Endurance cyclist Jay Petervary had shared these thoughts when asked about his upcoming attempt at the Tour Divide. The race is the world's longest off-pavement cycling route. It travels through Alberta, British Columbia, Montana, Idaho, Wyoming, and Colorado before finishing in Antelope Wells, New Mexico. According to the Tour Divide website, by the end of the 2,745-mile route, a through-rider will climb nearly 200,000 vertical feet, equivalent to summiting Mount Everest from sea level seven times.

Petervary's answer was in response to the interviewer's question regarding Jay's goals for the race. He mentioned two goals specifically that I remember. One was to set a new record, which would require a Herculean effort to best fifteen days and was ultimately beyond the cyclist's control. Untimely rains or late snowmelt can mean hours, if not days, of pushing the bike. What Jay could control would be his other goal of going to a place he'd never been before. The place he spoke of was not geographic in nature. It lives within each of us. It is the stuff of creation, stamped on our DNA. If we are awake and honoring this life for the gift it is, then whether in business, family, or adventure, we are constantly looking for our next "better." If one is to believe that as human beings we are without limit, which I definitely do, then it follows that our soul would constantly be in search of the next challenge that would provide such an opportunity.

This pursuit of being your best also eliminates the debilitating effects of comparison. Years later, I'd have the great honor of sharing the stage with retired four-star general Tommy Franks, honoring members of the Iowa National Guard at their annual gala, both of us invited speakers. He closed his speech that day with these words: "The world doesn't need another Nelson Mandela or Martin Luther King, Jr. What the world needs is the very best version of you." There is no competition, no comparison with anyone in this effort. If you do everything with all you've got, then from this day forward, you'll win. Someone will always be faster, jump higher, be smarter, or have better hair, but did they give all they had with all they were given? Who knows? Hopefully, yes. This race called life is only against yourself.

I've followed Jay's career from the day I first saw that interview. He has become a friend and mentor. I'm a fan of anyone, anywhere, with the stones to look fear in the face and take on a challenge when they are uncertain of the outcome. They are my teachers, my inspiration to keep pushing the envelope until the day the lights go out.

Chapter 63

A THIN SERPENTINE PLUME OF SMOKE ROSE ABOVE THE TREE-lined shore. I couldn't be sure of where it was coming from, though I bet I'd know its exact location sooner versus later.

There was a good chance the small fire wasn't even on the river. It could be campers a bit inland or racers who had decided to bivvy, needing a break from this winding, rainy, cold purgatory called the Yukon River Quest. I longed for the dense fog in my mind to clear, for just the slightest sliver of light to poke through and provide a positive thought, a ray of hope. I couldn't remember the last time I had mustered as much as a smile. During the gnarliest of times in adventures past, I'd always force a smile, reasoning that my suffering would suck a bit less if I could at least smile. Try as I may, nothing would come at that moment. My thoughts were not negative; they were simply void. I'd passed through negativity, denial, and all forms of positive and negative mental self-wrestling. Despair? No, I was beyond even that. There was only emptiness. If any paddling were going on, it was not due to my conscious effort to do so. I was of no more consequence to the river than a piece of deadfall that had finally relented in its battle against gravity and the forces of nature and fallen into the river. Its battle now done, with nothing left, it would float without purpose as the river saw fit. As would I.

The great river began arcing slowly to the left. My paddle found its way into the water back left so as to guide the boat through the turn. There were no thoughts of *What next? How much further? Can I? Can't I?* There were no thoughts at all.

Clearing the bend, my head lifting just enough to see what lie ahead, the source of the smoke was revealed.

To this day, I don't know what that place was. Had I made it to the Little Salmon checkpoint, or was this just some random safety check that I was unaware of? I guess I probably inquired upon pulling my kayak onto shore. Whatever the response was, I have no recollection.

I knew, however, exactly what this place meant to me. I had reached a place I had never gone before. There would be no beyond.

I was done.

Chapter 64

BEATEN DOWN BY A FULL NIGHT OF RAIN, THE FIRE ALSO HAD lost its battle. The coals were still hot enough to produce heat, though, and that bit of smoke that had guided me here. It was evidence of a fire that had recently burned hot and bright—just like me.

The last of the strength that I possessed allowed me to pull the kayak safely out of the river. The thud of the craft was easily audible. Unable to lower it gently onto the shore, I simply let go of the rubber handle tethered to the front of the kayak. My right hand, all too happy to be rid of the burden, just opened without as much as a thought and let it drop without any concern. It deserved better.

The few steps up the bank I'm not even sure were taken in succession. Everest climbers speak off how, upon getting within arm's reach of the summit, a distance of ten meters takes minutes, each step the result of the last plus a minute or two of rest to gather the resolve to take the next.

The small tree stump that sat in wait next to the smoldering fire was my mountaintop, and the bank of the Yukon River was my mountain. I desperately wanted to park my ass on that piece of wood; it was all that remained of the tree that had once stood proudly on these banks before meeting its demise at the hands of some northern logger. The incline was no more than a few degrees, and the distance was no more than twenty meters, so I thought, *To hell with it. I'm going to curl up in a ball on the bank and go to sleep forever.* What a sight I must have been, trudging, stopping to take a break on my pilgrimage to the log seat, expressionless, bent at the waist in an attempt to continue on.

To my memory, the man who met me there was a burly, barrel-chested, bearded fellow, though I cannot be certain of any recollections from that point forward. All memories are as clouded as the dreary skyline that had been our reality for many days past.

To his credit, he would not accept my muddled, half-coherent, "I'm done man. No more...I got nothing."

Perhaps the old boy had himself paddled this evil demon of a race before and knew the place I was in. Or maybe I was not the first shell of a human that had passed through. Or maybe he was simply a tough man who called this tough land home and, like all others I had met this past week, had compassion and caring for anyone who came here to take the test. Maybe it's just in the blood of those who call the rugged places home. They look out for each other. Support each other. Help in any way they can. It was a takeaway lesson from Whitehorse. It was a village. No one seemed any greater or lesser than anyone else, and they were all very proud of this place they called home.

"Let's get your stuff laid out by the fire and get something warm inside of you."

If that meant retracing my steps to the kayak to retrieve all the gear that had been soaked in my efforts to not drown, I'd rather just sit on the log and die. Walking back to the kayak was not an option, and I couldn't really give a shit about getting my clothes dry. I wasn't getting back in that boat. *Maybe this well-meaning lumberjack of a man had a hearing problem,* I thought.

With the gentleness of a den mother, he extended his hand. He helped me the last few feet to the log seat I'd had my sights on since exiting the kayak.

"Let's get you back with the living, buddy."

Draping a giant old patchwork wool blanket over my shoulders, he left me to bathe in the warmth of the coals. He returned moments later with a jacket, socks, a stocking cap, and underlayers in hand. Without the desire or ability to as much as lift my head, I followed his movements only as far as my eyeballs moving back and forth would allow.

"Start working on this."

It didn't seem like much time had passed, but out of the kayak, draped in the blanket, I believe his statement woke me out of a sleep. He gave me chicken broth, perhaps, but I'm not entirely sure. Registering barely as pleasant, it didn't have the effect I would have guessed. For so many hours I had only wanted to be rid of that damn kayak and be warm. Now here I sat, on the world's most wonderful piece of wood, legs free to stretch out—or not—as I wish. A wool blanket that probably cost the coats of a whole damn herd of sheep based on its size and warm chicken broth were not working the way I had envisioned. No one was home. I was empty. I could recognize the coals, the blanket, and the broth as things that were warm, but I just couldn't feel them. If he had asked me, "Are they warm?" I would have answered "Yes, they are warm, but they aren't making me warm." To describe it is difficult. I wasn't cold anymore. I wasn't warm either. Slumped over, head in hands on that log along the shores of the Yukon River, I was nothing.

Time ceased to exist. The clouds would not clear; the sunlight was not returning. If anything, it seemed like everything was slowly continuing to darken. I was barely aware of where I was as the waters of the Yukon River flowed past without me.

"I can't go any further."

I'm unsure if my Yukon caretaker heard me or if I even said the words aloud. I'm not certain if we had been in conversation, or if I was responding to a query as to how I was doing. I only remember his hand finding my knee.

"Everything's gonna be alright, buddy. I've called the rescue boat. It will be here soon. You hang in there."

Chapter 65

IT HAD BEEN NEARLY A DAY SINCE THE BULLET HAD EXITED THE barrel of the gun. For almost twenty-four hours it had sailed through the air until finally finding its target. The moment I found myself upside down in the Yukon River was the moment the trigger had been pulled.

Once "safely" back on terra firma after self-rescuing in Lake Laberge, I'd needed to put on every single layer of dry clothing I owned to stave off impending hypothermia. Incessant rain, drizzle, cold temperatures, and wind eventually penetrated them all, finding my vulnerable skin. The bullet had been gaining speed, closing in, and I had had no idea. A fraction of a degree, imperceptible to the senses, left my body, again and again...and again. Its cunning, the manner in which it took its time debilitating its prey—me—was genius. Never had a bullet travelled so slowly yet still packed such a wallop.

To the educated or alert observer, I imagine my manifesting symptoms would have been noticeable many hours prior. By the time my keeper at the mystery checkpoint recognized I was in trouble, the bullet had already found me. The damage had already been done. Now a different clock was ticking. If this one struck zero, I would not avoid the hangman a second time.

The Mayo Clinic website lists the signs and symptoms of hypothermia as shivering; slurred speech or mumbling; slow, shallow breathing; weak pulse; clumsiness or lack of coordination; drowsiness or very low energy; confusion or memory loss; and loss of consciousness.

Eight symptoms. I had checked seven out of the eight boxes. At that moment, able only to nod in the affirmative to the information that the rescue boat had been called, I displayed all but the shivering. My body was shutting itself down in an attempt to keep all my major organs functioning. Like I had been the past hour in my kayak, unable to muster even the weakest stroke of the paddle, I was once again just along for the ride. Not once did I realize the extent of the trouble I was in. I was too dull to monitor my own bodily functions. My life was no longer my own. I'd live or die based on the caring, expertise, and efforts of others.

I had no sense of time. Vaguely, I heard something about a few hours. Fortunately, the boat was near. During prerace meetings, we were told immediate rescue was not a guarantee. Had others been in the queue needing help, it could have taken much longer. Time, looking back, that I would not have had.

My caretaker spoke up, "Time to go. Boat's here."

I don't know how I got to the boat. It's all a blur, a mix of what I think are real images and faint recollections of conversations I had or that took place around me.

I do remember being helped into the big orange emergency jumpsuit. *It's so heavy*, I thought. Its warmth should have provided comfort. It did not. It seemed like more of a straitjacket then any real help. I wanted out of the damn thing.

"Sit down. Get out of the wind and keep it zipped up," the captain barked.

"How long is the ride gonna be?" I tried to yell, hoping to be heard over the loud engines that had us screaming down the Yukon River. It was the next to last thing I recall about the ride.

I was startled awake.

"Hey! Hey! Drink this. We're almost there."

I was confused. Where was here? I drank. It was hot. Not burn-your-mouth hot, but hot. It tasted like crap. Black coffee seemingly filtered through an old gold rushers sock. Immediately, away I drifted.

Coming to a stop woke me again. Someone hastily made their way into the boat as the boat's captain helped get me off the boat. It all seemed over-dramatic.

What was the big deal? I wondered, not even half-alert, or maybe not even half-alive. It seemed by their actions and tone that I was the only one not in touch with the gravity of the situation. A few steps off the boat, the lights went out. Did I pass out and lose consciousness, or had my system just shut down another bodily function in an attempt to preserve the life still hanging on inside?

Events, thoughts, and the details of all things had been crystal clear during my fight in Lake Laberge. The split second it had taken to roll, realizing I was going under, had taken place in slow motion. *Oh no! You're going over, dude! Deep breath. The water's gonna be freezing, so don't gasp for air no matter what once you tip or you'll drown instantly swallowing the water. This is gonna suuuuuck!* I can remember the entire discourse as clearly as the waters of the river were. It all happened in the time it took to flip upside down. The water had been freezing, shockingly so, but my self-rescue training had got me past the first hurdle; my lungs were still full of air, not water. Panic had set in, though, as I searched frantically for the spray skirt release before accepting my fate. Accepting that this would be the place my life would end and feeling the peace that acceptance provided, I had been able to gain the composure to open my eyes, find the handle, and set myself free. All those details were crystal clear.

Now, inside the medical tent, things were not so clear. I was a spectator in an unfolding drama, viewing it all from somewhere between life and death. The reception was poor, both audio and visual. All that was clear was the seriousness of it all; there were people making a fuss, something like, "Get all those clothes off him, now!" This was followed by more hurried, deliberate movements and instructions. Then, snap—like that, the screen went blank. Reception gone. Show over.

Chapter 66

SOMETIMES YOU WAKE FROM A SLEEP SO DEEP YOU'RE LEFT COMpletely disoriented. *Where the heck am I?* you think. It takes time to sort reality from dream and, on occasion, to even parse your current location. That was what I was experiencing upon my return to the living. Being unable to move without struggle served to add to the disorientation of the situation. My limbs were so heavy. It seemed I was entombed in blankets, with layers and layers of wool both above and below.

Where am I? What happened? Questions swirled while I did a quick systems check. My head was pounding with an enormous headache. My mouth was dry as a bone in the desert; swallowing felt like I'd attempted to eat an empty Pepsi bottle, its glass shards now embedded throughout my throat.

"You gave us a pretty good scare, buddy."

The details of the exchange still remain hazy. I'm guessing the lady who had kept watch over me was a nurse or perhaps an EMT. The canvas tent "door" swung open, revealing a bit of light, which answered my subconscious question of whether it was day or night.

"Hey there, buddy" another woman exclaimed upon entering. "Great to see you awake."

I wondered, silently at first and then asking louder, to the best of my ability, beckoning my keeper closer, "What happened? Where am I? What day is it?"

Caringly, she pulled up a seat next to the army-style cot I lay upon and shared the details of the past twenty or so hours.

What?!

Nearly a day had passed without my having any sense of it since I had been carried from the rescue boat to the place where I now lay. I listened as best as I could, though most of her words were lost in the pain in my head and throat, and the rest struggled to pierce the dense fog that impeded my brain's ability to see or discern anything clearly.

Then, out of the fog, a thought emerged from the haze, blinding in its clarity. All pain, all discomforts, all questions, for a moment, were gone.

I had failed.

I had travelled great distances, invested great time and effort and what little money I had, to take on the Race to the Midnight Sun. The World's Longest Kayak Race. The Yukon River Quest. And I had failed. I'd failed friends, failed relatives, failed acquaintances, and failed every well-wisher, known and unknown. I'd failed myself.

Or had I?

Katie Swales, a local resident of Whitehorse who had become as much a friend as someone could during my brief stay in town prior to the race, was one of the many awesome volunteers assisting to make the race and the area so amazing. Eventually, gathering first my wits the best I could and then my clothes, now dry thanks to those who had kept watch over me, it became necessary to figure out how to get back to Whitehorse. Katie offered a ride forward to Dawson City, explaining how cool it was to see racers finish and the festivities around it all. I had no doubts about the truth of what she was saying, but if I was ever to see Dawson City it was gonna be from the seat of a kayak, not a pickup. She understood.

Eventually, we loaded into her truck and began our back-track to Whitehorse. I wasn't much for chit-chat. For one thing, my throat wanted nothing to do with it. For another, there was a whole lot of mental processing going on. The winding road seemed to follow the great river, although I couldn't be sure. My gaze continued out the passenger's side window. I had plenty of time to think. I'd paddled that damn kayak a long way from the start. Even by motor vehicle, it would take some hours before we'd arrive in Whitehorse.

The drive was good medicine. Not so much for the physical ills—that healing would take days, perhaps longer. But the spiritual hurt? With each turn of the highway taken, each hill crested, the beauty of this harsh place began to resuscitate my soul. Disappointment gave way to introspection. The Yukon. This beautiful, rugged, harsh land offered one item in spades: truth. She had opened her arms to me, revealing herself. No bullshit. Only truth. She offers a test to all who come to her seeking. Be it a fortune in gold, a desire to live simply, carving out a life in one of the true remaining frontiers, or a kayak race, she welcomes all. She does not, however, relent. Care as she may, her love is a tough love. Some found riches in her hills; some died trying. Some were able to make this place home, some failed, and some found a measure of what they journeyed here in search of. Some would paddle into Dawson City as conquering kings and queens of the Yukon. Others, like me, would not. I suspect the creator of this place neither rejoiced nor shed a tear for any of us.

I imagined her joy coming from the simplicity and the purity of this place. Joy, sadness, disappointment, elation; these were what awaited all of us who came to this place searching for something uniquely personal.

I had been called to the Yukon. My soul, awakened years prior, yearned for the wild places. Like the wolves that called this place home, it wanted to howl alone in the darkness, calling to the moon above. Its song pierced the night air, giving notice to all of its complete freedom, its unwillingness to be bound by society's all-too-often accepted constraints.

Dawson City and the finish line of the World's Longest Kayak Race, the Race to the Midnight Sun, the Yukon River Quest, had eluded me. But not before I had faced death, standing on its doorstep twice. In turn, I had gained a deeper understanding of life and of how I would live it from this day forward. I had given this place all I had, and she had done the same for me.

Perhaps someday I would return. Still glancing out the window, I smiled. Just a bit.

Author's Note

WHAT DOES IT MEAN TO ME THAT YOU HAVE TAKEN THE TIME TO read *Upside Down in the Yukon River* or my first book, *Forty Days*? It means that you are a part of my journey.

It has often been said that nothing great is ever accomplished alone. I believe that to be true, and my life experience bears it out. I am nothing unto myself. I don't mean to imply that either of my books rise to the level of great prose, but I can tell you this: they were written to the absolute best of my ability.

I am ordinary in every sense of the word. There is nothing exceptional in my makeup, except perhaps that I am an extraordinary dreamer and a believer in the possibility of all things. I have learned the value of taking the crucial first step on a journey, armed with the knowledge of where I am headed and trusting that though I may not have it all figured out at the start, the answers will come along the way.

The universe supports those who dare. It conspires to our—to *your*—greatness. It is my hope that somewhere in these pages you have found inspiration to take the first step on your own journey: start that new business, take that dream trip, be that all-star parent, or just get the hell off the couch. Don't wait! Time, like toothpaste, can never be put back in the tube. Procrastination is the killer of dreams. If we do not do what we cannot do, there is no problem; but if we do not do all that we can, then we have wasted the gift of life. The world does not need another Nelson Mandela, another Martin Luther King, Jr., Mother Teresa, or Mahatma Gandhi.

What the world does need is the very best version of each of us—the very best version of you.

With my most sincere gratitude and respect for your time, I thank you for reading *Upside Down in the Yukon River* and becoming a part of my life journey.

Adventurously yours,
Steve

About the Author

STEVE CANNON RUNS, FAT BIKES, KAYAKS, AND SKIS. HE WOULDN'T call himself a runner, biker, kayaker, or skier, however; he mostly refers to himself as an adventurer. In 2018, Steve completed his greatest challenge to date: the Iditarod Trail Invitational 350 in Alaska, one of the top ten extreme ultra-endurance races in the world.

He has completed the Tuscobia Winter Ultra 150 twice on his fat bike. He has three Arrowhead Ultra 135 finishes and in 2018 did so "unsupported," meaning all food and water was carried from start to finish. In 2016, Steve earned an induction into the Order of the Hrimthurs, the Triple Crown for winter ultra-endurance athletes.

In 2004, he rode his bike to the starting line of the Deadwood Mickelson Trail Marathon in South Dakota—beginning in Iowa—before running the marathon. He has completed the Register's Annual Great Bicycle Ride Across Iowa (RAGBRAI) more than twenty times, the Ride the Rockies five times, and the Dirty Kanza 200, the world's premier gravel cycling race, five times, earning a coveted "1,000 Miles of Kanza" goblet in 2017.

He has run nearly 100 marathons. He ran 292 miles across his home state of Iowa in eleven days and is the first person ever to run around the Lake Michigan, logging 1,037 miles in forty days—averaging a marathon's distance per day. This adventure and its lessons became his first book, *40 Days: Life, Love, Loss and A Historic Run Around One of the World's Largest Lakes* (2015).

His adventures have raised nearly $700,000 for Livestrong, Camp Kesem, and Above and Beyond Cancer.

To learn more about Steve Cannon, follow his adventures, inquire about him speaking at your next event, or participate in one of his online courses, visit www.expandyourpossible.com. You can find him on Instagram, Twitter, and Snapchat (@xpandyourpossible) or Facebook.

CPSIA information can be obtained
at www.ICGtesting.com
Printed in the USA
FSHW022003090421
80353FS